Empowerment through STEM education

Barbara J. Adams

TABLE OF CONTENTS

Page

LIST OF TABLES

DEDICATION

ACKNOWLEDGEMENTS

ABSTRACT

Chapter One: Study Introduction 1

    Background and History 1
    Computer Science 3
    Need for Research 7
    Previous Research 8
    Statement of The Problem 9
    Statement of The Purpose 10
    Research Questions 10
    Methodology 10
    Theoretical Perspective 11
    Significance of the Study 12
    Summary 12

Chapter Two: Background and Related Literature 14

    Overview 14
    Women in the Computer Science Landscape 15
    The Numbers 15
    Participation and Community 16
    Gender and Culture 18
    Engagement Practices Framework 26
    Informal Engagement Practices 27
    Formal Engagement 36
    Increasing Female Representation 46
    Opportunities for Systemic Change in Undergraduate CS Programs 48
    How Current Research Differs from Previous Studies 50
    Summary 51

Chapter Three: Research Methodology 53

    Overview 53
    Restatement of the Research Questions 53
    Qualitative Research Design 53
    Researcher's Role 55
    Sampling Strategy 57
    Participation 58

Plan for Data Collection 58

Data Analysis Procedures 60
Validity and Reliability of the Data Gathering Instruments 64
Protection of Human Subjects and Ethical Considerations 66
Participants 66
Participant Descriptions 68
Summary 70

Chapter Four: Results 72

Restatement of the Research Questions 72
Modifications Based on Pilot Interviews 72
Answers to the Research Questions 73
Recommendations for encouraging participation. 90
Reasons for Persisting 94
Summary 100

Chapter Five: Conclusions and Suggestions for Future Research and Action 102

Discussion of Key Findings 102
Strengths and Limitations 113
Recommendations for Practitioners 114
Recommendations for Future Research 117
Implications 119
Closing Thoughts 120
Conclusions 121

LIST OF TABLES

Page

Table 1. Theme Definitions..72

Table 2. Demographics for Participants in Order of First Interview.............................77

Table 3. Key Experiences for Women in a Computer Engineering Undergraduate
  Program...83

Table 4. Factors that Make Undergraduate Computer Science Departments Effective Spaces for
  Encouraging the Participation of Female Students..84

Table 5. Factors that Make Undergraduate Computer Science Departments Ineffective Spaces
  for Encouraging the Participation of Female Students..93

Table 6. Types of Experiences that Encourage Participation by a Diverse Group of Female
  Students in Undergraduate Computer Science Departments............................96

Table 7. Types of Experiences that Discourage Participation by a Diverse Group of Female
  Students in Undergraduate Computer Science Departments............................99

Table 8. Recommendations for Young Women Pursuing Computer Science and Engineering..102

Table 9. Reasons for persisting in Computer Science and Engineering....................104

Table 10. Supportive Male Peer Behavior..107

Table 11. Outside Supports..110

DEDICATION

To all of the young women and other underrepresented people pursuing technology-related degrees and careers– so that you can continue to pursue and persist in the field. And, to Oscar, Estela, Gabi, Avelina, and Daniel.

ACKNOWLEDGEMENTS

Thank you to everyone who has inspired my love of learning including my mentors, parents, sister, coaches, and teachers. Special thanks to C20, Judi Fusco, Linda Polin, and Patti Schank.

ABSTRACT

Women continue to be underrepresented in computer science and technology related fields despite their significant contributions. The lack of diversity in technology related fields is problematic as it can result in the perpetuation of negative stereotypes and closed-minded, unchecked biases. As technology tools become integral to our daily lives it is essential that a diverse group of people contribute to the sociocultural environments where we participate and live. This dissertation is a phenomenological, interview-based, study designed to investigate the lived experience of women in undergraduate computer science and engineering programs. The purpose of this study was to better understand the factors that might encourage or discourage the participation women in the major and in the field. In order to grow the number of women in technical fields it is important to first understand what attracts them to the field and what supports they find helpful or not helpful.

This study illuminated some recommendations that might guide the work of practitioners in secondary schools as well as higher education. Among other things, participants appreciated being challenged by the content and assignments, feeling support from faculty and peers, feeling a connection to the culture, effective encouragement to persist, and engaging interactions. All of the participants described having gone into their field to make a positive impact on society and they also all described the importance having at least one supportive female mentor. Participants described the importance of having spaces where they felt included and appreciated their professors and peers who pushed back against the historical CS-world stereotypes. While the experience of each participant was unique, and there were some very negative experiences, all six participants reported having mostly positive experience in their undergraduate programs.

Chapter One: Study Introduction

To be a woman in tech is to know the thrill of participating in one of the most transformative revolutions humankind has known, to experience the crystalline satisfaction of finding an elegant solution to an algorithmic challenge, to want to throw the monitor out the window in frustration with a bug and, later, to do a happy dance in a chair while finally fixing it. To be a woman in tech is also to always and forever be faced with skepticism that I do and feel all those things authentically enough to truly belong. There is always a jury, and it's always still out. (Lee, 2017, para. 13)

Background and History

While women have made significant contributions to the field of computer science (CS), they are often not acknowledged and are currently underrepresented in the field. For example, *Newsweek* recently published a special issue entitled *The Founding Fathers of Silicon Valley* which depicted seven white males on the cover. This issue reflects the popular historical narrative of Silicon Valley. In response to this special issue, Jessi Hempel wrote *A Women's History of Silicon Valley* where she challenged that narrative and described the lack of historical representation as a barrier that precludes women from entering the technology industry. Hempel (2016) shared the stories of women in Silicon Valley that often go untold including the stories of: Judy Estrin, Lynn Conway, Sandy Kurtzig, Donna Dubinsky, Sandy Lerner, Diane Greene. The seventh spot on the list was marked "XXXXX" and represented the women whose names have been forgotten or who have gone unrecognized. It was an attempt by the author to acknowledge the, as she put it: "many people of different backgrounds who go unrepresented in Silicon Valley's popular historical narratives" (Hempel, 2016, para. 35).

Gürer (2002) found that textbooks that summarize the history of computer science also document few women. Notable female computer scientists include Ada Lovelace, Grace Hopper, the World War II "computers," Judy (Levenson) Clapp, Thelma Estrin, Margaret Hamilton, Sister Mary Kenneth Keller, and many others. In spite of their substantial contributions to the field, current participation by women in undergraduate CS programs in the United States is significantly lower than that of their male counterparts. Women only earn 18% of all computer and information science undergraduate degrees (Koch & Gorges, 2016). In addition, women's underrepresentation in computer science in recent years is widely documented (Beyer, 2014). As described by Wilson, Sudol, Stephenson, and Stehlik (2010), the computer science pipeline is broken. The problem is two-fold: first, there are not enough computer science students in the United States to keep up with the country's need for highly skilled computer scientists; second, women are an underrepresented group in computer science departments, and are underrepresented in industry as well (Gal-Ezer & Stephenson, 2009).

The National Science Board (2016) recently published a report titled Science and Engineering (S&E) Indicators that points to the historical underrepresentation of women and members of several racial and ethnic minority groups in S&E work. This low representation suggests an underutilization of human capital for S&E work and research. While the number of women with S&E degrees or in S&E occupations has doubled over the past two decades, the disparity is still pronounced. The National Science Board (2016) found that while women constituted 50% of the college-educated workforce overall, they only constituted 29% of workers in S&E occupations with or without an S&E degree. Among S&E degree holders, women represented 39% of employed individuals in the field. In computer engineering, women account for only 11 to 12% of the workforce. In computer science, they account for 25% of the workforce. Although the number of women in computer science occupations has doubled since 1990, there are still many more men than women. As the field has grown, the proportion of women in the field has decreased from 31% to 25%; male participation has doubled – growing 188% between 1993 and 2013 (National Science Board, 2016). Hamdan (2015) reports that a low ratio of women to men in CS-related professional positions is the result of discrimination from men, other women, and self-discrimination. Gender stereotypes threaten women in male-dominant work. Being a lone woman, or one of very few, leads to not having company on her team and feelings of isolation; this, in turn, can, end up affecting her performance and success in the field.

As technology tools become integral to our daily lives it is essential that both women and men learn to program the tools that contribute to the sociocultural environment where we participate and live. These tools, after all, are transforming the way we learn, work, and live (National Science Foundation, 2014). All people need to be able to use the tools available to them in robust ways. More importantly, all people should be welcomed to participate in the process of creating such tools, and in designing and programming them. A diverse team is more likely to consider the appropriate affordances for a wide audience. For example, early releases of Apple's iPhone Health App allowed users to track scores of self-entered health measures, but ignored one of the most commonly tracked data for women: menstruation. As Phillips (2014) describes, a more diverse population can lead to more innovation as people with different backgrounds work together. In addition, individuals of different genders, ethnicities, and backgrounds have different needs and experiences; tools made by only one person or group might not necessarily be as applicable or useful to individuals in other groups and others may need different tools. It is important to ensure that differences of opinion and perspectives are represented within the teams that develop the tools we use every day.

Computer Science

As this research focuses on computer science education, it is important to first describe computer science. As illustrated in Lewis and Smith (2005), computer science scholars have long examined the question "What is computer science?" Pea and Kurland (1984) defined computer science as "that set of activities involved in developing a reusable product consisting of a series of written instructions that make a computer accomplish some task" (p. 5). Gal-ezer and Harel (1998) described CS as a new science with connections to other fields including engineering, mathematics, and physics. According to Denning and McGettrick (2005), most computing people understand computer science to mean programming, information theory, and complexity; after all, half of the recent Association of Computing Machinery (ACM) A.M. Turing Award winners have contributed to the field of CS in the areas of complexity, theory, and programming. This, they argue, has led to a too narrow view of the field and a communication gap between those who want to use computing technology and those who make it. In an effort to narrow this gap, the ACM created the Computer Science Teachers Association (CSTA) and endorsed experiments to find curriculum modifications that could express computing as a broad and appealing field to a larger number of people. The ACM K-12 Task Force Curriculum Committee (2003) presented a broader definition of computer science: "the study of computers and algorithmic processes, including their principles, their hardware and software designs, their applications, and their impact on society" (p. 6). More recently, Parlante (2005) described computer science as a spectrum with science, or traditional mathematical-algorithmic research on one end and engineering, or the techniques and challenges of building complex systems on the other. Parlante (2005) argues that software projects as a whole include islands of pure algorithm integrated into a larger ocean of system complexity. Accordingly, computer science refers to a fluency in both algorithms and engineering (Parlante, 2005; Salton, 1972).

When computers became more popular and educational institutions and employers needed to train programmers, programming aptitude measures were employed to identify programmer trainees. The Programmer Aptitude Battery was developed in 1950s by IBM to identify future employees (Pea & Kurland, 1984). Instead of approaching computer science education from a variety of pedagogical approaches, it was more cost effective to employ a fixed approach and allow the belief that there was an aptitude for computer science to endure while those who were not seen as having an aptitude for CS were not considered to have the "right stuff." Pea and Kurland (1984) identified several issues with this approach and foresaw the lack of diversity that would result if new pedagogical approaches did not allow for an equal opportunity to learn about and participate in the computing world – a world that they were certain would continue to have a large impact on education, business and society. Instead of asking the question of whether the aptitude variables contribute to success in programming, Pea and Kurland (1984) identified the need to focus first on identifying the purpose and goals of programming.

Computer science has a documented problem with the historical exclusion of women in the U.S. and other countries (Mellstrom, 2009). One reason for this might be that men placed themselves in central positions in the history of CS and the field became associated with masculine values in the U.S and some other countries. There is a disparity in female and male students' attitudes and opinions about computer science culture (Stoilescu & Egodawatte, 2010). However, this is not a universal problem and in countries including Malaysia, Greece, and Turkey, there is strong female participation in CS (Adams & Rapids, 2003; Mellstrom, 2009). The under-representation of women in computer science, then, seems to be a problem limited to specific countries and cultures. In order to grow the number of women in CS and engineering positions in the United States, it is important to understand what attracts women to CS and why they choose to persist in the major.

CS in higher education. Having been developed in the 1940s, the computer brought with it concerns around who should control it and whether the hardware belonged in math, engineering, or science (Brackett, Nestman, & Spees, 1978). Other questions included whether theory or application should be paramount, what applications were most important, and where computer science fit in a liberal arts curriculum. In an effort to address some of these questions and propose the development of an undergraduate curriculum in the new field of computer science, the ACM began meeting in the 1960s. Researchers including Brackett, Nestman, and Spees (1978) began to advocate for the continued use of technology as a way to improve life, and called for the liberal arts to begin to use technology to improve the human condition through social change by embedding computer science in all facets of the liberal arts curriculum.

Lewis and Smith (2005) recognized an ongoing identity challenge with respect to the role of CS within the university community. The researchers presented a conceptual framework that examined the identity challenge recognized from three computer science perspectives: the segregationist, the integrationist, and the synergist perspectives. The segregationist perspective defines CS in terms of algorithmic analysis and theory building, and limits the development of curriculum to CS faculty and administration. The integrationist perspective sees CS as being driven by industry and sees CS courses as needing to be driven by the needs of the computing masses; integrationists invite other disciplines to the table to integrate CS curriculum. The synergist paradigm integrates both segregationist and integrationist perspectives and defines computer science by its ability to be flexible to the demands of all stakeholders when developing curriculum. Of the three perspectives, Lewis and Smith (2005) advocated for the synergist paradigm in order to ensure that the field will survive and thrive. According to Lewis and Smith (2005), curriculum should be developed with contributions from both internal stakeholders — CS faculty and administrators — and external stakeholders — graduate schools, parents, industry and other departments. The synergist perspective, then, embraced the perspectives of all stakeholders in the development of computer science curriculum. Moreover, the synergist paradigm asserts that computer science is defined and strengthened by diversity and constant innovation (Lewis & Smith, 2005).

    The synergist perspective, which combines instructionist and constructivist pedagogical approaches, is described by Lewis and Smith (2005) as an all-inclusive philosophy or approach. The researchers encourage a synergist perspective and predict that the future of CS departments depends on their ability to embrace this synergistic, social exchange, approach. In university CS departments, the synergist perspective involves engaging all stakeholders in CS education including students, parents, graduate schools, industry and other university departments. The perspective is consistent with the ideas about the importance of diverse design teams in industry presented above. Including more stakeholders in CS education by adopting a synergist perspective might be an important step in supporting the inclusion and participation of all types of people in CS including women and other underrepresented minorities.

Need for Research

In order to increase female participation at all stages of CS education and industry, it is important to understand the whole picture of the lived experience of women in undergraduate programs. The underrepresentation of women in CS is an important topic for equity reasons as well as economic ones (Beyer, 2014). A recent National Science Board (2016) report points out that policymakers have increasingly emphasized the need to expand CS capabilities in order to keep up with the demand for employees in technology industries in the United States.

With respect to women in CS, Wang et al. (2015) found that most of the decision-making for young women who choose to pursue CS-related fields occurs before they begin college, because upon entering, the requirements for college CS classes can become a barrier. Further, many of the factors that play a role in a young woman's decision to pursue a CS-related field are largely controllable. The researchers found that the top four factors influencing young women to pursue computer science include social encouragement, career perceptions, academic exposure, and self-perception. Family plays a critical role in the encouragement and exposure that young women get, and outreach to parents is a way to support young women entering computer science and related fields. Encouragement and exposure to the field can be provided by anyone, and play a large role in influencing young women to pursue a computer science degree. Even seeing representations of female role models in the media, can encourage a young woman to pursue CS-related degrees. It is important for young women to see representations of people who look like them in the field and to have real-life female mentors and peers who can support them in their pursuit of CS-related degrees and careers. The actionability of some of the factors described above, then, allows educators and others to positively influence and encourage young women in high school to pursue CS degrees in college (Wang et al., 2015).

This study is highly relevant to furthering an understanding of the factors, controllable or uncontrollable, that might influence a young woman's decision to pursue a Bachelor of Science in Computer Science and Engineering (CSE) degree. The study seeks to understand the whole picture of the lived experience of the female CSE undergraduate student, including the individual, her family, and academic, social, and career perceptions as factors that contribute to the lived experience of a woman in CSE. This study also investigates why participants decided to major in computer science and engineering and whether the *Engagement Practices Framework* identified by Monge, Fadjo, Quinn, and Barker (2015) to address areas key to retention of undergraduate women and minorities in CS is being applied to support their participation. By examining these factors and current participation structures, the researcher hopes to gain a better understanding of the participation of women and how learning interactions happen among students. It is important to note that like most fields of study, a spectrum of academic programs include computer science practices. This study focuses specifically on a computer science and engineering program.

Previous Research

A wealth of information on the participation of women and other underrepresented groups in computer science and engineering is available in the research. Scholars tend to focus in several areas including gender differences, curricular adjustments, the sociocultural environment of CS-related undergraduate programs, and factors that influence the participation of women and other underrepresented groups. For example, Stoilescu and Egodawatte (2011) studied the level of resources, instruction, and CS culture-specific knowledge of women when compared to their male peers. The researchers found that instruction and culture-specific (ie. CS-world) knowledge were areas where a digital divide was detectable and pervasive. In other words, computer-based instruction and pedagogy does not give regular and effective access to women. Also, women reported being less able to access the computing culture in their undergraduate computer science programs.

Nasir and Vakil (2017) studied how STEM learning spaces and access to those spaces are tied up in notions of identity, race, gender, and a sense of belonging. Other researchers identify issues with CS curriculum specifically including the insufficient exposure to ethical, moral, and social issues in the use of computing in society. Social stereotypes that stem from prejudice and discrimination persist, and an environment that fosters learning for all has been called on to address this deep-rooted problem (Fisher & Margolis, 2002). Another wave of research has examined the broader impacts of the interventions implemented by Carnegie Melon University and reported in Fisher and Margolis (2002). The interventions presented included addressing culture, curriculum context, prior curriculum experience, support through pedagogy and faculty relationships, and support through building awareness and confidence. Buffum et al. (2016) discuss the importance of reaching out to all students who do not have access or existing influences to study computer science, and studied in-school pre-secondary initiatives to support efforts to broaden participation for all. Certainly, there are various studies that approach the problem of participation from a range of angles. In contrast, this study seeks to better understand the many factors that contribute to the lived experience of the female CSE undergraduate student and the effects of that experience on the student.

Statement of The Problem

Broadening participation by women in an industry where they have been traditionally underrepresented is essential to transform CS-related fields into spaces where all feel included. Furthermore, populations are better served by the technology products that are developed as a result of more inclusive team. As Gürer (2002) described in her article – originally printed in 1995 – despite not being mentioned in standard CS textbooks, women have made significant contributions to computer science and engineering. Pioneering women were involved in original work both technically and theoretically (Gürer, 2002).

In order to increase the participation of women in undergraduate CS-related programs, it is essential to have a better understanding of the lived experience of females who are currently participating in those programs and why they do so. This study is a small step towards better understanding the lived experience of females in undergraduate CSE programs in the United States. Understanding the experience of current students might lead to a better understanding of how to attract and support women in their pursuit of CS-related programs at the undergraduate, graduate, and industry levels.

Statement of The Purpose

The purpose of this phenomenological study is to investigate the experiences of female computer science and engineering majors in college to better understand their participation in the field. Specifically, this study examines the factors might encourage or discourage the participation of young women in undergraduate CS-related programs.

Research Questions

- What are the lived experiences of female undergraduate computer science and engineering majors?
- What makes undergraduate computer science and engineering departments effective or ineffective spaces for encouraging the participation of female students?
- What types of experiences encourage or discourage participation by a diverse group of female students in undergraduate computer science and engineering departments?

Methodology

This study used a phenomenological approach. Phenomenological research seeks to describe experiences from the perspective of the participants. Individuals are the unit of analysis of phenomenological studies and data are collected almost exclusively through interviews (Gray, 2014). In this study, six undergraduate women majoring in CS were interviewed remotely, using video conferencing technology. The interviews were transcribed and characterized using a methodology called interpretative phenomenological analysis (IPA). The study examined the lived experience of the participants as well as whether a framework called the Engagement Practices Framework (EPF) as being applied to support women's participation in their undergraduate CS community. IPA and EPF are described in more detail, below.

Theoretical Perspective

This study seeks to understand the experiences of female undergraduates within their undergraduate computer science departments. Phenomenology allows the researcher to describe the experiences of people and to bring to light both what is really present as well as what is imagined as present in their experiences; both the real and the ideal (Moustakas, 2016). As described by Smith (2004), the particulars of a case can be described as containing a fundamental quality that brings us closer to understanding aspects of a shared experience. The principles of phenomenology and specifically interpretative phenomenological analysis (IPA), are integrated throughout the research design of this study in order to accurately represent the experiences of its participants. IPA is a qualitative research approach that seeks to understand the participants' personal lived experience and how they make sense of their experience (Smith, 2004). To understand the undergraduate experiences of women in CS departments, several elements will be examined in the literature review: PreK-12 and undergraduate formal and informal education practices, the computer science culture, female identity, recruitment and retention of women in CS, and proposals for intervention.

This phenomenological study, seeks to understand the practice of undergraduate CS education. While phenomenological research does not lend itself to a theoretical framework, the literature reviewed in Chapter 2 serves as a foundation for understanding the phenomenon involving female undergraduate CS majors and their experiences in a major where they are the minority. Smith (2004) describes reality as fuzzy, and points to IPA as a method of analysis that systematically makes formal theoretical connections after the textual analysis of an interview is done. Data for this study was collected from interviewing six undergraduate women majoring in CS. Themes were developed through the inductive research techniques described by Smith (2004), which are flexible in allowing for unanticipated topics and themes to emerge during the data analysis process. The formal theoretical connections for this study emerged and were guided by the analysis of the transcripts of the interviews. This emergent process built on the foundation of the literature review, helped define the parameters of the research project, and guided the data analysis process.

Significance of the Study

Broadening participation in CS through engaging women in the discipline is essential for increasing the number of participants in both CS education as well as in CS careers. This study is meant to illustrate the current experiences of women in computer science programs at universities in the United States as a way to better understand the factors that might encourage or discourage their participation and persistence as undergraduate CS majors.

This study began with a review of the existing literature to get as sense of what is currently understood about the lived experience of female CS undergraduates. The results of this study support the current research in the field that identifies social encouragement, family support, career perceptions, academic exposure, and self-perception as the leading factors that influence women to pursue computer science (Wang et al., 2015). It also supports research that points to culture, curriculum context, prior curriculum experience, support through pedagogy and faculty relationships, and support through building awareness and confidence as elements that encourage continued participation for women in the undergraduate environment (Fisher & Margolis, 2002). The findings of this study also illuminate some specific strategies for exposing women to CS-related fields and for supporting women as they pursue a CSE degree in college.

The identification of actionable factors that might positively influence and encourage young women to pursue CS-related degrees in college is of particular interest to the researcher, a secondary school CS educator. After all, as described by Wang et al. (2015), most of the decision-making process for young women pursuing CS and related fields occurs before she begins college.

Summary

This study seeks to bring to light the lived experience of women pursuing undergraduate CSE degrees. It will examine the whole picture of participation and persistence of female computer science degree seekers in college and consider the strategies that they identified as supporting or not supporting their participation in an undergraduate CSE program. Chapter 2 discusses the existing literature on factors that influence the participation and persistence of women in computer science, specifically in undergraduate computer science departments. Chapter 3 presents the research design, data collection techniques, data recording techniques. It also addresses relevant concerns regarding the use of human subjects for the study. Chapter 4 describes the results of this study on the lived experience of young women in undergraduate computer science and engineering programs. Chapter 5 discuss the significance of the results of the study and makes recommendations for further study.

Chapter Two: Background and Related Literature

Overview

This study investigated the lived experience of female undergraduates in the field of computer science and engineering to understand what they are faced with as women in a major where, in most computer science departments in the United States, they have traditionally been underrepresented.

Since the 1990s a great deal of effort has been dedicated to improving female participation in computer science. However, women continue to make up only 18% of computer science majors in college (Patitsas, 2016). The low participation in undergraduate programs has significant equity and industry implications (Wang, Hong, Ravitz, & Ivory, 2015). As explained by Margolis, Goode, and Chapman (2015), access to computer science (CS) is a civil rights issue because technological advances are needed for social good but more time and capital is being spent on making violent and misogynistic video games. Not only that, but CS is impacting the entire world through technological advances in fields like medicine, environment, health, literacy, and humanitarian causes (Margolis, Goode, & Chapman, 2015). It is essential that those who sit at the design tables and those who lead technology projects and companies represent the diverse perspectives and the needs of our population as a whole. As such, access to CS classes and programs for diverse populations is essential in developing active and informed citizens of the world who can actively participate in a democracy. Increasing women's participation in computer science is a critical workforce and equity concern. The opportunities for women and other currently underrepresented groups in CS and technical fields is extraordinary (Frieze, Quesenberry, Kemp, & Velázquez, 2011).

As described by Margolis, Goode, and Chapman (2015), equity in computer science must be monitored constantly to ensure progress and a narrowing of the current race and gender gap in the field. Computer science education for all students is an essential step in ensuring that the social needs of our world are addressed in an equitable fashion. In order to decrease the race and gender gap for the industry as a whole, it is important to increase awareness of CS through exposure, encouragement, and support (Wang, Hong, Ravitz, & Ivory, 2015).

While there is a broad range of literature in the field of computer science and women, this study will center on elements of the literature that examine the participation of women in computer science from high school through early career. Although this literature review will largely focus on academic participation in computer science, the implications for professional positions in computer science and the barriers to participation in the community of practice will also be explored, as one purpose of education is to gain access to jobs and contribute to society. The latter half of the chapter will explore factors that influence participation in computer science for women as well as efforts to broaden participation for women in computer science through systemic changes. The chapter concludes with a description of how the research project will draw from previous research efforts and extend work done previously.

Women in the Computer Science Landscape

The technology industry has committed to reversing the negative trends for women in computer science and other computing fields (Wang, Hong, Ravitz, and Ivory, 2015). Current research efforts have examined societal, cultural, and psychological reasons for the underrepresentation of females in the academic computer science landscape in the United States (Patitsas, 2016; Wang, Hong, Ravitz, & Ivory, 2015). Recently, Patitsas (2016) found that some CS departments are once again restricting access to their majors and classes. These admissions and computer science department policies have a profound impact on how many women study undergraduate computer science. This research adds a political dimension to understanding the computer science landscape and culture.

The Numbers

Between 1994 and 2004, there was a large variation in the representation of women receiving CS degrees at US liberal arts institutions (Richards, 2009). Out of a total of 92 schools studied the average percentage of CS degrees granted to women ranged from 5% to 31% among degrees awarded to women undergraduates. Other recent studies of female participation in undergraduate CS programs make clear that the percentage of females is low (Beck, 2007; Margolis, Fisher, & Miller, 1999; Patitsas, 2016; Wang, Hong, Ravitz, & Ivory, 2015; Wilson, 2002). For example, Patitsas (2016) reported that women continue to make up only 18% of computer science majors in college. Similarly, Wilson (2002) found that females accounted for only 18% of the total number of participants enrolled in six sections of and introductory CS course, CS 202, at a comprehensive midwestern university. CS 202 was chosen because it is the first programming class required in the computer science major sequence. Beck (2007) shows that at Truman State University, for the academic years 1996-2000, approximately 63% of undergraduate students were female, but only 18% of incoming freshmen computer science majors were female. Additionally, approximately 60% of the women who entered the university as CS majors (18%) did not complete a CS baccalaureate degree (Beck, 2007). The research literature points to a persistent concern about the low numbers of females who enroll in college CS courses. The low number of female participants at the undergraduate level leads to low participation at each subsequent level of the CS "pipeline", which in turn suffers from "leakage" due to four social factors. According to Wilson (2002), those four social factors include a lack of parental encouragement, a widening male female peer group gap, stereotyped game software mainly directed at males, and a lack of female role models both in the classroom and on television or in public spaces. Additionally, as Salter and Blodgett (2012) documented, there are strong anti-feminine and anti-feminist sentiments in gaming culture. While only one part of CS-related work, the video game industry is sometimes described as one where systemic sexism structures exist (Chess & Shaw, 2015).

Participation and Community

An examination of culture gave an insightful and effective approach in trying to understand women's participation in computer science at Carnegie Mellon University (CMU)

(Frieze, Quesenberry, Kemp, & Velázquez, 2011). Research on the attitudes of CS majors at CMU showed that the Women-CS cultural fit can be strong in undergraduate environments. The phrase Women-CS cultural fit describes the researchers' findings that women can fit successfully into a CS environment alongside their male peers. It benefits everyone to have women and men in an undergraduate CS environment helping to shape the cultural landscape that they participate and learn in. Most importantly, Frieze, Quesenberry, Kemp, and Velázquez (2011) found that this reshaping of CS culture by both women and men not only improves the Women-CS cultural fit but it also benefits everyone without compromising the academic integrity of the program. These findings are consistent with current research in the field of diversity. Solving problems with people who have different information, opinions, and perspectives is beneficial for all (Phillips, 2014). As described by Phillips (2014), a female engineer might have different perspectives than a male engineer, adding to informational diversity. Just like interdisciplinary teams are essential when building things like a car, socially diverse groups also add value and correlate to better performance in CS (Phillips, 2014).

From a sociocultural learning perspective, social diversity is a positive force since learning and thinking are situated in the culture and setting in which they happen. Williams (as cited in Frieze, Quesenberry, Kemp, & Velázquez, 2011) defined culture as the synergistic process of change by which we shape and are shaped by the cultures we occupy. Extending that definition of culture presented by Williams, Cole (1998) described culture as a system of artifacts within which things and tools can grow. Cole used the garden metaphor to describe the environment created to support the growth of certain plants. The garden, then, links the "micro-worlds" of individual plants with the "macro-world" of the external environment. The internal system of activity or interactions will interact with a larger system, just like students in undergraduate CS environments will eventually move from the undergraduate "garden" into graduate school or industry "gardens."

Culture emerges as a group engages in activity together over a period of time (Cole, 1998). The reshaping of CS culture, through increasing the participation of underrepresented groups in the CS community, benefits everyone and is in the interest of the computing world (Frieze, Quesenberry, Kemp, & Velázquez, 2011).

Blaney and Stout (2017) identify a need for more research examining the experiences of women in the computer science classroom. Specifically, the researchers described a gap in the literature that exists in seeking to understand affective experiences of women and the degree to which they feel a sense of belonging, inclusion, and valued as members of the academic computer science landscape. After all, researchers identify both self-efficacy and a sense of belonging as elements that promote positive academic performance and motivation in computer science.

Gender and Culture

Stoilescu and McDougall (2011) identify a gender divide in CS through a focus on gender differences and a stereotype where females and males alike view computer science as a male domain. These computing related gender stereotypes are consistent with those previously illustrated by Fisher and Margolis (2002). Current scholarly research on gender stereotypes in CS draws on the work of researchers from Epstein (1988) to Fine (2010) who argue that theoretical frameworks like essentialism, the attribution of fixed characteristics to females and males, are the result of embedded social structures and not inherent differences in gender. Fine (2010) examined psychology and neuroscience literature to discredit the idea that there are hardwired differences between the brains of women and men. Rather than being *hardwired*, the brain changes and responds depending on a variety of factors as one goes through life. As reported by Newcombe (2007), attempting to account for biological causation of sex differences have not been successful. In their analysis of sociocultural and biological considerations with respect to the underrepresentation of women in CS-related fields, Ceci, Williams, and Barnett (2009) described attempts to establish a biological disadvantage for women as littered with *loopholes* including poor reasoning and unsupported arguments. Biological evidence, they argue, is "contradictory and inconclusive" (Ceci, Williams, & Barnett, 2009, p.218).

Cohoon (2003) and Fine (2010) describe an equal number of women and men participating in computer science departments internationally in countries like the Republic of Armenia and some former Soviet Republics, discrediting the essentialist idea of an inherent female characteristic that accounts for the underrepresentation of women in the discipline. Furthermore, gender is often constructed differently in different cultures, clearly showing that attributes ascribed as natural to men and women are products of local culture, not necessarily gender (Frieze, Quesenberry, Kemp, & Velázquez, 2011). For example, Fine (2010) describes greater gender segregation of occupational interest in advanced industrial societies rather than in developing ones like Armenia, where women in CS make up about half of CS majors.

Unfortunately, gender stereotypes persist in the United States CS culture and they serve as gatekeepers to the CS landscape, depriving underrepresented groups, the computer science field, and society at large of the benefits of diversity in a community (Fine, 2010; Koch, Gorges, 2016; Page, 2008; Stoilescu & McDougall, 2011). By taking a cultural approach to understanding women's participation in CS in the U.S., an essentialist view of participation is rejected (Frieze, Quesenberry, Kemp, & Velázquez, 2011).

The cultural approach to broadening participation for women in CS was a direct response to the lack of explanation that a gender difference approach was able to provide for the decreased participation of women in CS and other technical fields. As a result of studying faculty approachability, environment, social fit, academic fit, and ingredients for success in higher education, researchers provide evidence that cultural and environmental factors play critical roles in determining women's participation in CS (Frieze, Quesenberry, Kemp, & Velázquez, 2011). Regardless of gender, all students deserve access to formal and informal opportunities to learn CS (Stoilescu & McDougall, 2011).

The intersection of gender and culture. It is important to consider the role of experience, environment, and culture in human development and learning (Fine, 2010). A benefit to assuming a cultural perspective is that it allows researchers to study factors outside of gender as contributors to different levels of participation by women in the micro-cultures of undergraduate computer science departments (Frieze, Quesenberry, Kemp, & Velázquez, 2011). As described by Koch, Lundh, and Harris (2015), sociocultural influences play a role in the participation of urban teenage African American and Latina girls across settings. Sociocultural influences can include adults who provide emotional encouragement, role models who connect girls to the CS culture, computing resources and materials, after school activities, internships, and the ability to build social-capital across setting (Koch, Lundh, & Harris, 2015). Furthermore, there is an interplay among the settings where a young woman participates: home, school, and after school settings. Research points to the need to develop greater opportunities for girls and their parents to connect to CS-related learning opportunities as a way of engaging not just the young woman, but also her support network in the opportunities afforded by CS (Koch, Lundh, & Harris, 2015). This interplay among settings where women participate and their connection to the CS culture will be discussed in more detail in the sections below in the Informal and Formal Practices in CS sections.

Perceptions of and related to CS. Researchers have found common perceptions of CS culture by teenagers and undergraduates who characterize computer science as boring, antisocial, and irrelevant to their lives (Hartness, 2011; Yardi & Bruckman, 2007). While these are not necessarily gender-based, they include the views of girls and women. In a study of teenagers, Yardi and Bruckman (2007) found that many of them expressed enjoying the affordances of technology including games and social networks. However, they perceive that CS careers are filled with lonely, endlessly detailed work, and the exclusion of under-represented groups. Furthermore, many of the teenagers interviewed by Yardi and Bruckman (2007) in an Atlanta after-school technology program assumed that they did not have the ability to manage the complexities of computer programming and careers associated with the field. To address this barrier, the researchers proposed a design-based curriculum to bridge the gap between teenagers' perceptions of computing and the opportunities that are offered in the discipline.

Similarly, Wang, et al., (2015) found that career perceptions were the second most potent factor influencing a high school girl's pursuit of CS. Stoilescu and Egodawatte (2010) described the mixed views about programming among female and male undergraduate students. Female students, they found, were more interested in the use of computers than in programming them. Male students, on the other hand, saw programming as a principal activity in computer science. Furthermore, men and women differ in the importance they place on goals related to work, marriage, family, and making a positive impact on society. Women felt that CS might impede their abilities to make a positive impact on society and spend time away from the computer due to the time required to be successful in the field. According to Wang, et al., (2015), understanding CS as a field with diverse applications and a broad potential for positive societal impacts is more important for women than men because of the value that women place on making positive impacts.

Another factor that influences participation in CS is a girl's interest in and perception of her proficiency in math and problem-solving skills (Wang et al., 2015). Researchers find that a positive self-perception provides internal encouragement which leads to confidence and interest in CS fields. Blaney and Stout (2017) report that both self-efficacy and a sense of belonging are key predictors of retention, persistence, and success in the computing field. These findings are consistent with the work of Bandura (1991) who described the choices that people make as closely related to their self-efficacy. In summary, it is the interests, confidence (or lack thereof), values, and personality characteristics that are often associated with gender that are the variables that need to be studied in order to understand CS course-taking by women (Beyer, 2014).

The computer science world. As described by Stoilescu and McDougall (2011), the influence of negative stereotypes about women in computer science has become a problem that needs to be addressed. Margolis, Fisher, and Miller (1999) described the "computer science world" as one that women are hesitant to join. Research in this area describes a computer science world that is male-oriented and has been referred to as hostile for women in part because social interaction and collaboration is often discouraged (Wilson, 2002). The world itself is described by researchers as one where status is determined based on programming speed and skills and membership in the culture depends on time spent in the terminal room (Margolis, Fisher, and Miller, 1999). Women in college CS environments described a male-dominated hacker subculture where there is an intense focus on the computer and spare time is spent programming, building robots, or reading CS books (Margolis, Fisher, & Miller, 1999; Wang, Hong, Ravitz, & Ivory, 2015). Beck (2007) reports that a majority of men in undergraduate CS programs describe themselves as computer nerds, geeks, and hackers. In contrast, the female participants in the same study did not describe themselves this way. The researchers reported the perception by women of this world as limiting and machine-centered. Furthermore, Cohoon (2003) illustrated the social context of CS departments as one that discourages women from going into CS using this quote from an anonymous computer consultant: "I guess life just isn't fair until women grow chest hair, spit, chew, bench press 250 pounds, and write a computer program." Similarly, Beck (2007) described the computer science education culture at universities in the U.S. as one that has been described as a male-oriented paradigm; one that presents a hurdle for women who, among other issues, do not see adequate female representation in the field.

In their longitudinal study, Margolis, Fisher, and Miller (1999) found that almost all of the female students who were admitted into the Carnegie Mellon School of Computer Science entered with high enthusiasm and interest. While both women and men were excited and passionate about the field of CS, the women interviewed by the researchers described their attraction to CS within the context of larger issues, often socially oriented ones. Many of the women reported their uncertainty in entering the computer science world because of their interests outside of just the computer and CS. A lack of interest in complete immersion into the traditional computer science world eroded the confidence and sense of belonging in the undergraduate CS community for some women leading them to doubt their belonging in the community (Margolis, Fisher, & Miller, 1999). The researchers also identified different orientations and elements that attract women and men to computer science; these will be described in more detail later in this chapter. These different orientations sometimes lead women to feel like imposters. Imposter behavior and thoughts and stereotype threat are described below.

Imposter behavior and thoughts. The *imposter phenomenon* (also referred to as *impostor phenomenon* or *imposter syndrome*) was first identified by Clance and Imes (1978) as a term used to refer to the internal experiences of a sample of high-achieving people who feel like "intellectual phonies." Fox, Ulgado, and Rosner (2015) described imposter syndrome as a person's inability to own their accomplishments. Other researchers have described the phenomenon as one whereby a person feels like she does not deserve her success and assigns it to external factors or to other people (Hamdam, 2015).

Falkner, Szabo, Michell, Szorenyi, and Thyer (2015) described a lack of a sense of belonging in computer science as well as a lack of positive identification with CS as elements that can lead to imposter behavior and thoughts. Imposter behavior and thoughts include a sense of fraudulence, where participants described not conforming to CS-related stereotypes and participants describing not believing that they were doing as well as their male counterparts. Both a lack of positive identification as well as a lack of a sense of belonging in CS relate to the stereotypes that have been found to undermine a woman's sense of belonging in the field. Exposure to the Gender Similarities Hypothesis can alleviate imposter behavior and thoughts.

Gender Similarities Hypothesis. Hyde (2016) recently described a prevalence of gender stereotypes in the United States and many other western nations that are not supported by current meta-analyses. The analysis of 46 meta-analyses, lead the author to propose the Gender Similarities Hypothesis which states that women and men are similar in most, but not all, psychological variables. Hyde (2016) began by outlining the work of Eleanor Maccoby in the 1970s that did not find evidence to support certain gender differences which were previously believed to be true. The work of Maccoby contradicted the previously held stereotypes including that girls excelled at rote learning while boys excelled at higher level cognitive tasks and were more analytic than girls. Recent meta-analyses show that women and men perform equally in mathematics assessments both in K-12 as well as in testing completed by adults. Small gender differences were described in verbal skills and moderate differences were found in 3D mental rotation. This in-depth analysis of 106 meta-analyses of cognitive and psychological qualities by the author therefore supports the Gender Similarities Hypothesis (2016). Education about this hypothesis, might mitigate imposter behavior and thoughts as well as support the mitigation of stereotype threat.

Stereotype threat. Steele and Aronson (1995) identified *stereotype threat* as the social-psychological predicament that can affect any group about whom negative stereotypes are widely known. The researchers studied the disruptive effects that wide-spread negative stereotypes can have in the academic performance of African American students taking tests. The researchers found that the existence of negative stereotypes about a group one belongs to can put someone at risk of confirming the stereotype to one's self and to others who know the stereotype (Steele & Aronson, 1995). Stereotype threat is the term used to described the phenomenon whereby stereotypes can produce performance impairment (Beyer, 2014; Steele & Aronson, 1995). For example, women who were reminded of the stereotype that there are gender differences in mathematics ability underperformed on math tasks when compared to women who did not receive the same message.

Beyer (2014) described gender incongruence for women in CS-related fields as undermining their sense of belonging in the field and consequently their performance. In the computer science and engineering academic landscape, women are consistently outnumbered by males by a ratio of at least 3 to 1. According to the National Science Foundation (NSF; 2017) report on Women, Minorities, and Persons with Disabilities in Science and Engineering, the number and proportion of women pursuing bachelor's degrees in science and engineering has declined over the past ten years. The proportion of women in computer sciences is highest at the master's level.

Cheryan, Siy, Vichayapai, Drury, and Kim (2011) describe male-dominated fields as being unwelcoming to women in two ways. The researchers describe that the skewed gender ratio can activate negative stereotypes about the abilities of women in the field and bring about their underperformance. This underperformance was found to be mitigated by female role models who have been found to protect women who are personally invested in STEM from the negative stereotypes and underperformance. Interestingly, negative gender stereotypes were found to be less threatening to women who are not invested in the STEM field (Cheryan, Siy, Vichayapai, Drury, & Kim, 2011). As a result of the low number of women in the field, mentors and role models for women are primarily men. While this can be problematic, it does not have to be. Cheryan et al. (2011) found that female and male mentors or role models in computing can help boost women's perceived ability to be successful if those role models are not perceived to conform to male-centered CS stereotypes. The gender of the role model, then, is less important than the extent to which that role model embodies current STEM stereotypes.

Stereotype threat only affects people who care about conforming to stereotypes. An example of this can be seen in experiments that were conducted with lower achieving female math students who were not bothered by their low achievement (Beilock, 2010). The scores of these young women did not suffer when they were told of the "girls can't do math" stereotype, possibly because they did not care about confirming the stereotype. In contrast, for young women who did care about their achievement, being reminded of the stereotype negatively affected their scores.

Stereotypes and women. In addition to the challenges of stereotype threat, young women can be deterred from pursuing CS-related degrees and careers by the stereotypes about the field that were described in the section above titled the computer science world (Stout & Camp, 2014). In their study of undergraduates, Cheryan, et al., (2011) found that STEM stereotypes pervade the media including sitcoms, commercials, and even on websites intended to encourage female participation in STEM. The researchers describe the proliferation of these stereotypes as unfortunate because they found them to prevent young women, who feel like they don't fit the stereotypes, from believing that they can achieve success in STEM. The same researchers found that interacting with just one member of a field, whether male or female, even briefly can contribute to a students' belief about their potential success within the field.

Schuster and Martiny (2017) studied negative competence-related stereotypes in undergraduate women. Their study is the first to document that in more stereotypical (i.e. male-dominated) contexts, women anticipate having fewer positive and more negative feelings suggesting to them that they will need to invest more time and energy than their male counterparts and might still feel a lack of belonging. The study found that women were driven away from STEM related careers more by the lack of anticipated positive feelings rather than by the increase in anticipated negative feelings. By extension, a less stereotypical context could provide women with more positive feeling, driving them toward STEM related careers. Schuster and Martiny (2017) described less stereotypical environments as ones where neutral language was used. For example, stereotype-activating cues include the term "ladies first" while a less stereotypical cue would be "you go first."

Engagement Practices Framework

Monge et al. (2015) described informal and formal practices that can have a positive impact on students in introductory CS classrooms. These practices have been organized into the *Engagement Practices Framework* and presented in several different ways (Barker, Cohoon, & Thompson, 2010; DuBow, Quinn, Townsend, Robinson, & Barr, 2016; Monge et al., 2015). Most recently, DuBow, Quinn, Townsend, Robinson, and Barr (2016) organize the *Engagement Practices Framework* into three research-based principles: (a) make the content matter, (b) grow positive student community, and (c) build student confidence and professional identity. These principles will be described throughout this paper and organized into the informal and formal practices that encourage or discourage the participation of women in CS. Informal engagement practices will be discussed next followed by formal engagement practices.

Informal Engagement Practices

Research suggests that informal CS-related experiences can be valuable opportunities for success for women as they allow them to participate, learn, and develop an interest in the field (Koch & Gorges, 2016). Monge et al. (2015) describe the following informal strategies as having a positive impact for engaging students: (a) effective encouragement; (b) mitigating stereotype threat; (c) encouraging student-to-student interaction; and (d) encouraging student-to-faculty interaction. Other informal supports that foster persistence particularly among urban teenage African American and Latina girls across settings include adult role models, encouragement from family and peers, and access to technology tools and CS-related programs (Koch & Gorges, 2016). These informal engagement practices (EPs) are described below.

Encouragement. Cohoon (2003) proposed that the lack of encouragement in CS is one explanation for why even women strong in mathematics were more likely to major in the humanities than in computer science. As Wang, Hong, Ravitz, and Ivory (2015) identify, social encouragement is one of the most powerful influences on the decision to pursue CS (discussed earlier in the section titled: *Perceptions of and related to CS*). Encouragement begins with the ability to participate in CS courses and activities. Both structured and unstructured ones can help increase participation in the CS field for women, especially if they take a CS course before college. It follows that exposure to and the ability to enroll in computer science courses in or out of school are critical to young women pursuing computer science in college. Monge et al. (2015) identify language that encourages students to persist through tasks in a CS course, and found that encouraging such language is an essential informal engagement practice that aids in the retention of women in introductory CS courses.

In an academic setting case study, NCWIT (2011) identified encouragement as a simple yet essential practice that requires positive communication and no additional resources. In a 2001 focus group, one woman reported that simply having teachers encourage her to pursue CS in college planted a seed in her mind about the possibility of engaging in the major. The student eventually realized she would find the major "fun" (NCWIT, 2011). In the same study, women reported that encouragement by faculty advisors helped them persist when they experienced moments of self-doubt. As described above, expressions of uncertainty are more likely to come from women due to society-wide stereotypes that undermine a belief in the technical competence of women.

With the goal of encouraging the participation of women at the undergraduate level, Cohoon (2003) found that actively recruiting women, encouraging them to persist in the major, and mentoring them to increase their representation in the major were particularly effective. Similarly, Wilson (2002) found that more females than males reported having been encouraged to study computer science in college. However, the low number of women pursuing CS-related degrees in college makes studying gender differences difficult. While Wilson proposes that if the encouragement were not there, the women in her study may not have chosen to study CS. Additionally, comfort level in the CS classroom was the best predictor of success in the course (Wilson, 2002). Wilson found a strong correlation between comfort level and self-efficacy and suggests that it is important for professors of CS to understand the importance of providing a classroom environment that encourages students to ask and answer questions both in and out of class.

Avoiding stereotypes. Avoiding stereotypes is another informal EP advocated by Monge et al. (2015). Developing curriculum that is free from stereotypes is a way to encourage participation by diverse groups of students in CS. Stoilescu and McDougall (2011) recommend giving the same informal and academic opportunities to females that their male counterparts have had access to. Gender, the researchers say, remains a stereotype that requires reflection. One strategy that Stoilescu and McDougall (2011) found to be successful in broadening female participation includes accepting a fixed number of females each year even when they might have less previous experience in CS than their male counterparts. This strategy is one way to minimize tokenization, the constant comparison that members of a minority might feel with one another, which is a struggle that female students might face being an underrepresented minority in CS classes. Similarly, providing counseling to both female applicants and registered students, raising awareness of the particular needs of female students and building a network of peers for female students were all reported to be effective strategies for supporting women in undergraduate CS courses (Stoilescu & McDougall, 2011).

Role of parents, mentors, and community. Margolis and Fischer (2002) described the role of parent and teacher expectations as a contributing factor for the underrepresentation of women in CS when those parents and teachers assumed that computing is boys work. This type of gender socialization has contributed to low engagement and interest in CS by women (Lee, 2015). The family of a young woman is a critical source of influence on her pursuit of a CS career (Koch, Lundh, & Harris, 2015; Wang, Hong, Ravitz, & Ivory, 2015). Key socializers including parents, adult family members, and community members play an essential role in encouraging and exposing young women to CS, which is an essential component in influencing their pursuit of CS and related fields (Koch & Gorges, 2016; Koch, Lundh, & Harris, 2015).

Closely tied to career perceptions is the positive influence that role models and mentors can have on women. Social engagement and positive reinforcement from family, teachers, and peers has a much stronger influence on participation for women than for men (Wang, Hong,

Ravitz, & Ivory, 2015). Young adults (both males and females) encouraged and exposed to CS by their parent(s) are more likely to persist in related careers (Wang et al., 2015). Women are also more likely than men to mention a parent as an influencer in their developing a positive perception of a CS-related field, more often citing fathers than mothers as the influencers (Sonnert, 2009). Unfortunately, parents' evaluation of their children's abilities to pursue CS-related fields differs by gender; parents of boys believe that their children like science more than parents of girls, more often overestimating their ability in the subject (Bhanot & Jovanovic, 2009). Family support is crucial for young women and was shown to account for 17% of explainable factors influencing a young woman's decision to pursue a CS-related degree. In addition, Wang et al. (2015) found that encouragement from non-family is almost as important, accounting for 11% of explainable factors influencing to a young woman's decision to pursue a CS related degree.

Sonnert (2009) argues that girls develop more positive perceptions of CS-related fields the closer their parents are to scientific professions. Wang, et al. (2015) echo this and show that providing opportunities for encouragement and exposure to the field of CS are key controllable indicators for whether or not young women decide to pursue a computing-related degree in college. As described by Wang et al. (2015), the influence on a young woman by family can be critical. Additionally, the researchers found that the encouragement can come from a family member or even a non-family member who does not have a technical background and still be effective. Lee (2015) describes parents and K-12 educators as having misperceptions about CS education. Misperceptions can result in a lack of awareness of the importance of CS education for all students. Wang et al. (2015) recommend that efforts to increase girls' interest in computing should include a parent education component that helps parents understand how they can actively encourage their daughters to participate in the CS landscape. This is especially true for parents who are not in technology-related fields (Wang, Hong, Ravitz, & Ivory, 2015).

Positive interactions with mentors is another way to encourage participation in CS by women. Clarke-Midura, Allan, and Close (2016), investigated the role of an all-female mentoring experience as a way to transcend barriers in CS with regard to negative stereotyping and lack of role models. While study focused on the benefits of the experience on the mentors themselves, both the high school girls who served as mentees and the paid near-peer mentors benefited from the experience. Near-peer mentors are "near" to the student in some way: age, ethnicity, interest, etc. (Ericson, Parker, & Engelman, 2016). Near peer mentors are described by Ericson, Parker, and Engelman as being in line with social learning theories that describe learning as a process that includes observing, imitating, and modeling what they learn from others who are "similar" to themselves. In their study, Clarke-Midura, Allan, and Close (2016) investigated the effects that participation in a paid mentorship program had on the mentors (high school girls). They found increased interest in CS and self-efficacy in the mentors. Their study did not look at the mentees.

Interest. A substantial amount of research has investigated factors that influence young women's interest in computer science (Fisher & Margolis, 2002; Stoilescu & McDougall, 2011; Wang, Hong, Ravitz, & Ivory, 2015; Yardi & Bruckman, 2007). Margolis, Fisher, and Miller (1999), pointed to the different interests and orientations in computing between female and male computer science undergraduate students. The researchers interviewed undergraduate students in the CMU computer science department and found that while most of the male students described an attraction to computers, nearly half of the women interviewed described their interest in computer science as attached to another area of interest including medicine, education, space exploration, and the arts. In other words, while males immersed themselves in the computer science world, the interests of women in CS did not detach them from people or social concerns; essential components of their identity (Margolis, Fisher, & Miller, 1999). Margolis, Fisher, and Miller (1999) described these problems as having been reported widely at other schools.

Beck (2007) found that women CS graduates and non-graduates reported problems with their social and academic environments. Stoilescu and McDougall (2011) explain that in addition to a reduced number of female students registered in computer science studies, female students feel isolated, have reduced confidence, and underperform their male peers.

Identity. Danielak, Gupta, and Elby (2014) described an undergraduate students' sense of belonging in a program as significantly affecting their decision to stay in engineering. The researchers argued for a closer examination of identity which is closely entangled with the approach a person takes towards learning. However, little is known about the intersecting social identities and experiences of women in CS-related fields, leading to limited success in increasing their participation and representation in the field (Blaney & Stout, 2017). Armstrong and Jovanovic (2017) describe these intersecting identities as being dynamically produced through social experiences. The researchers argue that issues pertaining to gender and equity need to be understood synergistically within the broader context within which the meaning of lived experiences is determined. For young women, that might mean considering multiple subordinate statuses that combine to shape their identity as well as their lived experience.

Sinclair and Kalvala (2015) describe the transition from school to university as a difficult one, particularly for women in CS who must deal with developing their identity within a predominantly male cohort. Identity is viewed as something that is constantly under construction as an individual interacts with others in social settings; identity is socially constructed and is a function of the role the individual plays in a community (Lave & Wenger, 1991; Riel & Polin, 2001; Sinclair & Kalvala, 2015). After all, learning is a process of identity transformation (Lave & Wenger, 1991; Riel & Polin, 2001). Undergraduate students are negotiating their identity in their undergraduate major communities as well as in the wider context of their university and society (Sinclair & Kalvala, 2015).

While stereotypical and societal identity roles affect CS participation, these should be challenged. Instead of catering to traditional gender differences and stereotypes, it might make sense to look for more meaningful efforts to encourage diversity, inclusion, and participation based on a range of characteristics, skills, and abilities, among other factors. Rethinking the CS curriculum so that all students are encouraged to develop and access a CS identity that resonates with them may be more productive than focusing on one gender (Sinclair & Kalvala, 2015). In developing such an inclusive type of curriculum, all students might feel welcomed and able to begin identifying as computer scientists.

CS-related learning environments. Outside of school, groups including Marcu et al. (2010), have held summer camps for junior high school girls where they encourage students to become engaged in engineering roles and creative projects. The researchers found that students became more engaged when they were required to present their work in a social setting. Creating an environment where students have fun with projects can make a significant difference in their attitude towards computer-related careers and can lead to increased participation (Frieze, Quesenberry, Kemp, & Velázquez, 2011; Hartness, 2011).

As described by Koch and Gorges (2016), after school programs can provide more equitable access to learning opportunities in CS-related fields than the opportunities offered in school. By providing hands-on, socially and culturally relevant activities, students have opportunities to engage positively in CS-related activities (Pinkard, Barron, & Martin, 2008). Furthermore, CS curriculum designed for informal learning environments can focus on specific ways of supporting and encouraging participation by women in CS (Koch & Gorges, 2012). Werner and Denning (2009) describe an after-school and summer program called Girls Creating Games where pair programming was determined to be a successful strategy for encouraging girls to engage with CS ideas. Learning environments that support metacognitive acts and encourage collaboration can support the persistence of girls in CS courses and careers as they learn to be resilient when faced with CS problems and challenges (Werner & Denning, 2009). In learning environments, mentors are also important; after school programs have also engaged middle and high school girls in computing through connecting them with near-peer mentors (Bartilla & Köppe, 2016; Clarke-Midura, Allan, & Close, 2016).

Faculty communities. As Beyer (2014) argues, encouragement from instructors is an important factor in retention in science courses. One resource developed by the National Center for Women & Information Technology (NCWIT) in collaboration with Google to support undergraduate CS faculty is the EngageCSEdu platform. This NCWIT project focuses on the impact that faculty can make in their role as teachers and provides resources to support this work. The EngageCSEdu platform also seeks to advance the *Engagement Practices Framework* and highlights teaching practices that have the biggest impact on recruiting and retaining women in CS majors. Part of the EngageCSEdu website provides a space for a community of CS faculty members to use, contribute, remix, and give feedback on the items in the collection (Quinn, 2015). EngageCSEdu is becoming a community of faculty committed to making teaching engaging and supporting women's meaningful participation in computing (Quinn, 2015). Online and face-to-face CS faculty communities both at the PreK-12 and University levels can foster communication and the sharing of materials, policies, and pedagogical strategies that can support improved educational experiences for all.

Undergraduate CS support groups for women. Positive student interactions and peer encouragement predict intention to major in CS among female community college students. (Beyer, 2014). Some universities have studied computer culture through support groups and clubs (Beck, 2007; Garcia, Ericson, Goode, & Lewis, 2012; Stoilescu & Egodawatte, 2010). Beck (2007) described significant differences in the activities that men and women have participated in prior to entering undergraduate CS programs. While women might enter their undergraduate programs with limited experience, men tend to enter with prior experience tinkering and otherwise "playing" with computers (Beck, 2007). But differences in prior experience are not typically addressed by CS departments. For example, Patitsas (2016) observed that diversity is not often considered in mainstream computer science department policy making, and "women's issues" are expected to be addressed by on-campus women's groups, not within departments. Nonetheless, Beck (2007) reports that undergraduate women's computer science support groups can provide significant benefits to female CS students. Key components of successful women's support groups are providing mentoring and outreach opportunities, emphasizing the social relevance of computing and the many industry and academic applications for a CS degree (Beck, 2007).

Schools like UC Berkeley have founded programs like CS KickStart as one-week intensive programs designed to recruit and support female freshmen who are interested in CS but have no prior experience (Garcia, Ericson, Goode, & Lewis, 2012). Support groups like CS KickStart begin to address some of the issues described by researchers including the lack of prior experience and exposure to CS that can lead to a disparity of participation between female and male computer science students in undergraduate programs (Stoilescu & Egodawatte, 2010). While these programs can have significant benefits, Beck (2007) concludes that without institutional support or faculty recognition efforts undergraduate women's CS support groups can fail.

DuBow et al. (2016) identified Association of Computing Machinery-Women (ACM-W) Student Chapters as communities where small groups of women from individual university classes can gather together and form a community with a critical mass. ACM-W Student Chapters are modeled after a standard ACM Student Chapter and focus on the particular needs of women through recruitment, retention, support, and celebration. At events sponsored by individual ACM-W Chapters, members can meet role models including peers and faculty members. Role models can serve as mentors and many ACM-W Chapters create formal mentoring programs for their members (DuBow et al., 2016). In addition to ACM-W Chapters, there is also the Grace Hopper Celebration for Women in Computing (GHC), which was created to celebrate the contributions of women in computing and technology (DuBow et al., 2016). Attended by students, academics, industry professionals, and government officials, the GHC supports the mission of retaining women in computing by providing attendees an opportunity to participate and learn with a community of women technologists.

Another group working in this space is the Anita Borg Institute (ABI). ABI initiatives include programs and communities to support women in computing. For example, "Systers" is an email community founded by Anita Borg and 12 other women in 1987 for women involved in computing and "ABI.Local" is a network of locally organized communities that bring women technologists together in cities around the world (Borg, n.d.; Frenkel, 1990). Both of these ABI communities are open to women of all ages and abilities.

Formal Engagement

Increasing access to K-12 computer science education has become an area of research in recent years. Research has shown that exposure to CS courses and activities, both structured and unstructured, can help increase participation in the CS field for women, especially if they have taken a CS course before college (Wang, Hong, Ravitz, & Ivory, 2015). Monge et al. (2015) describe the following formal strategies as having a positive impact for engaging students: (a) grouping students by experience level; (b) instructional strategies; (c) process oriented guided inquiry learning (POGIL); (d) student choice and inquiry-based learning; (e) worked examples; (f) student-focused assessment. These formal strategies discussed by Monge et al. (2015) as well as other formal engagement practices will be described in this section.

K-12 formal engagement opportunities. In the U.S., high schools that limit computer science education to courses like *Advanced Placement (AP) Computer Science A* fail to attract women and minorities (Webb, Repenning, and Koh, 2012). Stoilescu and McDougall (2011) identify the importance of increasing awareness and helping women see themselves as successful in computer science education as an important way of increasing participation by women in CS classes. In another effort to attract young women and minorities to CS, Webb, Repenning, and Koh (2012) call for a renewed vision for computer science pedagogy, that includes revising curriculum to help broaden its appeal and encourage more female participation.

Outreach efforts to encourage participation in K-12 CS education by women include a broad range of approaches ranging from the recruitment of computer science teachers and counselors to presenting what careers are available to graduates in CS (Hartness, 2011). As Frieze, Quesenberry, Kemp, and Velázquez (2011) examine, cultural and environmental factors play critical roles in determining women's participation in CS. A compulsory CS program in U.S. K-12 schools, for example, could go a long way towards ensuring that all students have access to computer science.

At the middle and high school level, one program that was developed and continues to expand is Exploring Computer Science (ECS). ECS is a curriculum designed and released in 2008 by Margolis, Goode, and Chapman (2015) to challenge persistent structural inequalities, widespread biased belief systems, and policies that combined to deny access and equitable computer science learning opportunities for females, African Americans, Latinxs[1] and other underrepresented groups of students. The ECS curriculum deliberately scaffolds units so that students from all backgrounds and abilities can enter the class and feel like they belong. Two other programs that target a broad range of students in middle and high school include *Bootstrap* and *Beauty and Joy of Computing* (BJC). Both courses are technically rigorous ones that include the teaching of higher order functions. BJC was chosen as one of the College Board's first five national pilots of the AP CS Principles course and is designed to be a rigorous, engaging, and broadly accessible course (Garcia, Ericson, Goode, & Lewis, 2012; Garcia et al., 2015). Bootstrap is a research-based computer science curriculum that reinforces algebra skills

---

[1] As defined in Wikitionary, Latinx is a gender-neutral word that replaces Latina, Latino, and Latin@ and is a way to refer to people who identify with Latin American racial backgrounds.

and geometric concepts and allows non-CS teachers to adopt materials and deliver rigorous and engaging lessons (Schanzer, Fisler, Krishnamurthi, & Felleisen, 2015).

While pre-college CS experiences are important, McGill, Decker, and Settle (2015) concluded that longitudinal studies need to be done to determine whether the countless hours spent on pre-college activities is effective across various groups. Knowing how different ethnicities participate in these activities and perceive their impact is essential in understanding how beneficial these programs are. In trying to understand the impact of pre-college and college interventions, it is important to also consider that in order for these programs to be successful, educators with extensive knowledge, experience, and expertise in the field must be available to teach courses (Gal-Ezer & Harel,1998). One benefit of the Bootstrap curriculum is the "gentle entry ramp" it creates for math teachers to begin teaching computing (Schanzer et. al, 2015). As schools seek to expand educational opportunities in CS, it is important to also consider increasing the pool of qualified CS teachers.

Undergraduate formal engagement opportunities. Undergraduate Computer Science and Engineering is a difficult major and the learning objectives that first-year undergraduate computer science students face are many. One of the issues is the curricular framework because, in many cases, students are not provided with enough time to develop the skills and knowledge that they need. For example, object-oriented programming requires a significant amount of time on task before students have sufficient facility with the approach to apply it to solve problems. Recent studies show that students who enter novice programming courses with prior programming experience perform significantly better than students who have no prior experience (Horton & Craig, 2015; Wilson & Shrock, 2001). Stoilescu and Egodawatte (2010) describe that lack of prior experience and exposure to CS is an issue that affects females more than males. As mentioned above, exposure to CS at the K-12 level might help address the issues described by Stoilescu and Egodawatte including the lack of prior experience and exposure to CS which can lead to a disparity of participation between female and male students in undergraduate CS.

Women in programming courses. Women in novice programming courses are put at a severe disadvantage. Excessively high workloads and courses designed with unachievable standards for novices are issues that disproportionately affect women given that more women than men choose to study programming in college with no prior programming experience (Luxton-Reilly, 2016). Furthermore, the low grades awarded in difficult first-year courses also discourage women more profoundly than men (Wolfe & Powell, 2015). Low grades in computer science are a result of a reliance on norm-referenced grading (grades based on performance relative to the class) as opposed to criterion-referenced grading (grades assigned without class reference). The use of norm-referenced grading has been found to turn students away from CS-related fields because they do not feel successful and it is not clear to them how they can improve. Grading will be addressed in more detail below in the section titled: *assessments, feedback, and potential fixes*. Low grades were found to discourage women, particularly minority women, more significantly than they discouraged men. In a study of low mean scores on CS-related assessments, Wolfe and Powell (2015) found that over 60% of the women found their low scores discouraging, compared to 15% of men who found them discouraging. These findings might partially explain the gender inequity and the lack of minority women observed in CS (Luxton-Reilly, 2016; Wolfe & Powell, 2015).

In addition to grades, another difficulty is the commonly held belief by computer science educators that programming is difficult to teach and learn, Luxton-Reilly (2016) asserted that almost anyone can learn to program when achievable expectations and standards are applied to student work. Shifting away from the "programming is hard" mindset to one that measures student work and progress against realistic expectations might have significant positive implications for women learning computer science. Luxton-Reilly (2016) argues that there is nothing intrinsically difficult in learning to program. The researcher argues that there is nothing intrinsic to the subject that makes it difficult to teach or learn and that the traditional view that programming is difficult to teach and learn may have negative implications for equity and diversity. Designing courses that expect too much from students is problematic and could potentially lead to undesirable behavior and a focus on student shortcomings as opposed to pedagogical or curriculum deficiencies (Luxton-Reilly, 2016).

Pedagogy. One way to support this shift is to employ resources such as those provided by NCWIT through the EngageCSEdu platform. In addition, Beyer (2014) found that both women and men want to take more CS courses when they have excellent instructors who design courses that apply sound pedagogical practices. Changes to pedagogical strategies may help bring gender pairity to undergraduate CS departments. Kelly (2008) proposes applying the Technological, Pedagogical, and Content Knowledge (TPACK) framework in a way that bridges issues surrounding the equitable access to technology, and advocates for pedagogical strategies that involve individuals as well as the learning community seeking answers to challenging and relevant questions. The curriculum adjustments recommended are grounded in the work of Vygotsky (1978) and Papert (1980) among others. Vygotsky described the value of scaffolding and the important role of more knowledgeable others in supporting the journey of a learner. Similarly, Papert's work, constructionism, explains the value of supporting learners as they build their own intellectual structures by adding elements that support construction. Brennan (2015) describes constructionism as grounded in the belief that the most effective learning experiences grow out of active construction, are developed through interactions with others, and support metacognition. Designing a constructionist learning environment, then, requires opportunities for students to engage with designing, personalizing, sharing, and reflecting (Brennan, 2015).

Understanding constructionism, however, is insufficient for teachers to understand how to translate these ideas into practice when designing learning experiences (Brennan, 2015). The EngageCSEdu website (mentioned above) attempts to help teachers apply these ideas by providing peer-reviewed and user-reviewed instructional materials focused on engaging students in introductory college and university CS classes (Quinn, 2015). The EngageCSEdu website also provides CS faculty with research-based techniques to engage students and it highlights the most engaging materials that employ at least one and often more than one of the engagement practices identified by the NCWIT Systemic Change Model for Undergraduate Computing Education and the EPs identified by Monge et al. (2015). By using the resources on the EngageCSEdu website, CS educators are employing teaching and learning strategies designed to engage all students to help make their courses pedagogically appropriate for all students (Monge et al., 2015).

Beyer (2014) described the value of pedagogically sound courses which are also engaging as critical for the recruitment and retention of female CS students. Beyer (2014) studied 1319 (872 female and 447 male) first-year US college students and concluded that evidence for gender differences in computer self-efficacy, stereotypes, interests, values, interpersonal orientation, and personality variables do exist. However, males and females alike were more likely to take more CS courses if they had positive experience in their first CS course. These factors predicted students' intentions to major in CS (as cited in Beyer, 2014). Wilson (2002) studied comfort level, math background, and attribution to luck as factors that might promote success in an introductory CS course. The researcher found that while there were no significant gender differences in the three factors studied, comfort level in the course was found to be a more important predictor of success than math background (Wilson, 2002).

Building positive student communities through pedagogy. Quinn (2015) identified techniques that contribute to building a positive student community engagement practice. The pedagogical techniques include structured and collaborative learning opportunities like pair programming and peer-led team instruction. Pair programming is a social pedagogy that has been shown to increase self-efficacy and interest among female computer science students (Clarke-Midura, Allan, & Close, 2016; Werner & Denning, 2009; Werner, Hanks, & McDowell,

2004). As described by Zarb and Hughes (2016), pair programming is a software development technique by which two programmers work side-by-side on the same computer to solve a problem together, taking turns with the keyboard so that one person (the driver) types while the other (the navigator) collaborates in the problem solving by checking for errors, looking up APIs, and thinking about better ways to structure the code. This technique is a beneficial pedagogical strategy for both novices and experts that often leads to greater enjoyment of the work at hand, increased engagement, and better quality code (Zarb & Hughes, 2016). Despite the benefits of pair programming, it can be difficult for novice programmers (as well as some expert programmers) because they have to learn collaboration strategies.

Pair programming requires collaboration rather than competition. Zarb and Hughes (2016) found that novice pair programmers benefit from the communication guidelines that outline what to do when the pair became stuck in a silent period, suggestions for planning periods, the importance of asking for clarification, and thinking aloud to help the partner understand how a task is being approached. In their study of pair programming by middle school girls, Werner and Denning (2009) found that while working with a partner, girls were engaging in exploratory talk involving metacognitive monitoring of themselves and their partners. Furthermore, this engagement in the debugging and problem solving process can have positive long-term effects on the persistence of females in the CS and engineering discipline. Building on previous studies, Werner and Denning describe the importance of girls developing resilience in the face of challenges if they are to persist in CS courses and careers. They describe pair programming as a technique that supports the development of successful collaboration and exploratory talk by girls, widening range of techniques they use when faced with programming challenges.

Webb, Repenning, and Koh (2012) propose a vision for CS pedagogy that focuses on another practice to engage learners: guided discovery sprinkled with just-in-time direct instruction. By demonstrating mastery of computational thinking concepts, students work both in the both Zone of Proximal Development described by Vygotsky (1978) and in the Flow condition described by Csikszentmihalyi (as cited in Webb, Repenning, & Koh, 2012); the researchers call this space the Zone of Proximal Flow. They report that such a guided discovery scaffolding approach motivated girls to learn CS. The principal element of guided discovery is teacher regulation of mediation in order to provide just the right assistance to support mastery of concepts. A guided discovery pedagogical approach, when compared to a directive approach, was found to address a motivational gap that had been previously identified between middle school girls and boys (Webb, Repenning, & Koh, 2012).

Other pedagogical techniques outlined by Quinn (2015) that contribute to building connections among students and help engage and retain women in computing include well-designed ice-breakers and grouping students by level of ability in order to build positive student communities in introductory CS courses. Quinn (2015) suggests providing opportunities for out of class interaction and creating welcoming informal spaces for all students.

Curriculum. Increasing the participation of female undergraduates in CS also requires a review of the current curriculum that is used in higher education. In an effort to counteract the deleterious effect that the image of CS and the "computer science world" has on female students, Carnegie Mellon University implemented several changes in their CS department curriculum (Margolis, Fisher, and Miller, 1999). The curriculum changes included: (a) an "immigration course" for new students to expose them to a wide variety of CS issues and applications; (b) interdisciplinary courses where students work on multifaceted problems; (c) a concentration in human computer interaction; (d) courses that focus on advanced computing applications; and (e) a new course that engages students with community groups that need CS support. The long-term goal of re-envisioning the CMU CS program was both to engage and educate more women, but also to broaden participation in a field that is currently very narrow (Margolis, Fisher, & Miller, 1999). Other research has shown that modifying curriculum in order to broaden participation through a design-based curriculum might bridge the gap between teenagers' perceptions of computing and the opportunities that are offered in the discipline. Yardi and Bruckman (2007) suggest that curriculum changes might motivate teenagers to pursue computing careers by presenting CS as an innovative, creative, and challenging field with real-world applications.

Assessments, feedback, and potential fixes. The Accreditation Board for Engineering and Technology now specifies that CS programs should evaluate students based on criterion-referenced grading norms (Wolfe & Powell, 2015). Criterion-referenced grading norms give students more meaningful feedback about the competencies that they have mastered and the ones that they have not yet mastered. Another practice outlined by Wolfe and Powell (2015) that might encourage broader participation involves reviewing the items students miss on exams in class so that exams can be informative to students in addition to measuring and classifying students.

The EngageCSEdu platform (described above) can support undergraduate CS educators in designing and using more effective assessments. The website hosts a collection of instructional materials aligned to the EPs Framework (described above), and provides a space where a community of CS faculty members numerous institutions can collaborate and share resources and practices (DuBow et al., 2016). For example, one resource shared on the site includes tips for implementing a *growth mindset* built on the work of Carol Dweck (National Center for Women & Information Technology, n.d.). Dweck (2006) describes a growth mindset as one in which learners view themselves as works in progress and recognize that their success is determined by how they approach problems in addition to their abilities. NCWIT and EngageCSEdu both provide resources for giving students effective feedback focused on learning through effort, practice, and feedback that encourages additional effort. EngageCSEdu will be discussed in other contexts later in this chapter.

McCracken et al. (2001) report on a curricular framework designed to be assessed through objective testing and performance-based assessment. That framework was developed by international experts and implemented at many universities. Objective testing includes both formative and summative assessments, including multiple-choice questions, that can provide instant feedback. Performance-based assessments include take-home programming assignments, examinations, and charrettes, which are short assignments completed in closed laboratory sessions. This curricular framework expects students to be able to: (a) abstract the problem from its description; (b) generate sub-problems; (c) transform sub-problems into sub-solutions; (d) de-compose the sub-solutions into a working program; and (e) evaluate and iterate (McCracken et al., 2001).

In their international multi-institutional study, McCracken et al. (2001) found that black-box student assessments might reinforce students' views of implementation and syntax as the key focus of computer programming. This study also points to poor programming habits in students due to the pedagogical approaches taken by their instructors. Furthermore, Luxton-Reilly (2016) proposes that there is a disconnect between the expectations of those who design CS curriculums and the capability of novice programmers. In particular, programming educators are systematically underestimating the cognitive difficulty of their curriculum and assessments for novice programmers. The disconnect between the cognitive difficulty and instructor expectations has implications for pass rates and grade distributions (Luxton-Reilly, 2016). As Lister (2010) demonstrated, grade distributions reflect both the students' programming ability and the methods that are used to grade them, and there are unrealistic expectations of student abilities in the first year of programming. As a result, poor grades might not indicate realistic performance.

Digital divides. One way to understand the difficulties that female students encounter in CS programs is to think about potential *digital divides* that can exist for learners including access to materials, access to computers, access to CS instruction, and access to the computing culture at their institution and the community at large. Medel and Pournaghshband (2017) describe established male-centered representation in computer science curriculum materials including imagery, language, examples, and other content. Stoilescu and McDougall (2011) used the three levels of digital divides identified by Kelly (2008) to explore gender specific challenges and barriers to participation by women in the computer science landscape in Western countries. Adopting a multidimensional approach, Kelly (2008) (and explained below) focused on technological pedagogical content knowledge (TPCK) for addressing issues of equitable access for students from diverse backgrounds.

The researcher describes the *first digital divide* as the presence of and access to equipment. The *second digital divide* is the access to achievement-enhancing technology mediated instruction both in and out of the classroom. The *third digital divide* is the access to technology mediated instruction that is culturally-sensitive and culturally-specific. Kelly (2008) proposes that each of the three digital divides can be bridged through a set of pedagogical practices that incorporate constructionism and social constructivism. These pedagogical practices will be discussed in more detail below.

In exploring the three layers of the digital divide, Stoilescu and McDougall (2011) noticed a difference between the experience of female and male students particularly with respect to the second and third layers of the divide: equitable instruction in computers and opportunities to foster computer culture. In their Canadian study, the researchers found high anxiety, a lack of confidence, and underachievement to be more prevalent in the women studied. In trying to understand the sociocultural stereotypes that could explain these differences, the researchers found that both female and male students identified computer science as a male domain. This means that males are better able to cross the third digital divide: computing culture (Stoilescu & McDougall, 2011). The researchers reported that female students also view CS as a hostile culture for females. Furthermore, male students were more active in classrooms and more likely to receive attention from teachers. Teachers who pay more attention to males are likely to be perpetuating the view that CS is a male domain.

Increasing Female Representation

Addressing the problem of underrepresentation of women pursuing degrees in computer science and engineering requires a multi-faceted approach. As described above, Monge et al. (2015) see the first courses taken by students in a major as a key intervention point. Women are less likely than men to declare a CS major when entering college, so their introductory course experiences can be especially important determinants of whether they will continue to take CS courses and possibly major in the field (Monge et al., 2015). Garcia, Ericson, Goode, and Lewis (2012) describe the call from Grady Booch to share the "passion, beauty, joy and awe" (PBJA) of computing with others as one way to address waning interest in computing in the United States. It is unclear if this approach is interesting to women, who tend to be more interested in the application of computer tools and methods in order to make a difference than the tools and methods themselves. Still, the PBJA "movement" was born out of an enrollment crisis and it is a valuable way to share best practices and advocate for teaching techniques that make computing fun.

Indeed, computer science education research points to a wide variety of factors that might promote success in introductory college CS courses. As described above, different undergraduate CS programs and courses have focused on specific factors to improve the courses. Some of those elements that have been studied as promoting success for both women and men in CS education environments include: adjustments to curriculum, assessments, exposure to the field, social encouragement, and comfort level (Fisher & Margolis, 2002; Wang, Hong, Ravitz, & Ivory, 2015; Wilson, 2002; Yardi & Bruckman, 2007).

Patitsas, Craig, and Easterbrook (2015) describe a process for scaling up efforts to increase the participation of women in CS education; they refer to it as the *Goldilocks process*. The researchers describe the large amount of time that CS educators spend on initiatives aimed at working with individuals and propose instead a sociological approach where change is initiated at the periphery instead. The *Goldilocks process* for making change happen is similar to the *Zone of Proximal Development* described by Vygotsky (1978), but instead of dealing with learning and growth at the individual level, the *Goldilocks process* deals with changes to a system. The researchers describe medium leverage changes as ones necessary in order to shift the system towards high-leverage changes by beginning to change behavior and function. For example, CS faculty members might evaluate and adjust their pedagogical approaches and classroom rules to ensure that they are not privileging certain groups over others. Once that change begins to gain traction, the shift continues and high-leverage changes become possible.

Opportunities for Systemic Change in Undergraduate CS Programs

In order to implement changes to a system it is important to first understand that system (Patitsas, Craig, & Easterbrook, 2015). While underrepresented groups in computer science and engineering have different reasons for their underrepresentation and encounter multiple biases, the scaling up of women in CS might also benefit other groups through system-wide changes (Patitsas, Craig, & Easterbrook, 2015). As argued by Stoilescu and McDougall (2011), a welcoming atmosphere in undergraduate CS programs could foster practices that support all in CS. To that end, Barker, Cohoon, and Thompson (2010) suggest the following as indicators of gender parity in an undergraduate CS departments:

- The percentage of undergraduate women in the department reflects the percentage of women undergraduates enrolled at the institution.
- Women are retained in the major at similar rates as men are.
- Women complete the degree in a similar amount of time as men do.
- The occupational choices of women and men are similar upon graduation.
- Participation in honors programs, research experiences, internships, and student groups, and extracurricular programs is similar in rate and roles taken on by women and men.
- The experiences of women and men as teaching assistants, lab monitors, and other positions in the department are similar.

The researchers describe the need for systemic reform in undergraduate computing designed to reach gender parity in the field. Building on the work by Barker, Cohoon, and Thompson (2010), the interdisciplinary team convened by Monge et al. (2015) operationalized a set of engagement practices to address areas key to retention of undergraduate women and minorities in CS. The researchers describe this work as essential due to their ethical commitment to diversity, and envision an improved future viability of the field through the innovation brought by diverse workers. The approach focuses on events and practices that women experience both directly and indirectly that might affect their outcomes, and the components of the model were derived from research on women in undergraduate CS programs and research on change in higher education. According to the researchers, the gender imbalance in undergraduate computing programs result from the way the current education system interacts with a variety of elements including the stereotypes that persist about the field and socialization that might inhibit participation by women.

The systemic change model was developed by Monge et al. (2015) as part of the researchers' work at the National Center for Women & Information Technology (NCWIT). With the goal of contributing to an improved educational experience for all, the model involves the following components: (a) recruitment, (b) pedagogy, (c) curriculum, (d) institutional policies, (e) evaluation, and (f) student support. These components of the model are elements which when manipulated can either promote or inhibit the participation of a diverse group of undergraduates. While each element can independently contribute to the promotion or inhibition of participation, the researchers argue that it is not enough to change one element in the system, but that undergraduate departments must address all of the elements of the model in order to promote diversity.

Additionally, the researchers describe teaching and learning strategies designed to engage students with a focus on pedagogy, curriculum, and student support. These engagement practices (EPs) fall into three categories, which were described above: students' perceptions of CS, students' experiences with CS through informal practices, and students' experiences with CS through formal practices (Monge et al., 2015). As described above, EngageCSEdu focuses on the impact that faculty can make in their role as teachers and seeks to advance the *Engagement Practices Framework,* which highlights the teaching practices that have the biggest impact on recruiting and retaining women in CS majors. To better understand the role that these principles play in setting up the conditions for a strong "Women-CS" cultural fit in undergraduate environments, it is important to understand the experiences of female undergraduate computer science majors. That is the primary goal of this study.

How Current Research Differs from Previous Studies

Reaching gender parity in the computing field and tech industry continues to be focus for groups like the NCWIT, ACM, CSTA, and ABI (DuBow et al., 2016). Re-envisioning undergraduate CS programs is one way of engaging and educating more women as a way of broadening participation in a field that is currently very narrow. While other research has investigated the influence of sociocultural contexts on a young woman in her pursuit of CS, further research is needed.

Research suggests that career thinking by young women is connected to their gender, ethnicity, race, and support networks – including family and parents (Koch, Lundh, & Harris, 2015). Koch and Gorges (2016) explain that researchers in CS-related learning spaces have begun to advocate for research that reaches across contexts to better understand how students are learning, persisting, and identifying with CS-related fields. Blaney and Stout (2017) identified a need to study the affective factors that might support the retention of women in the field of computer science. Falkner et al., (2015) interviewed CS academics and PhD students and their perceptions of the field of CS as well as how they see themselves within that field. However, few studies have explored the persistence of female students in computer science and engineering undergraduate programs and their support networks across contexts or their experiences within their departments (Koch, Lundh, & Harris, 2015). Understanding the quality of women's experiences in the classroom as well as outside of the classroom is important in order to have a more complete understanding of the representation of women in computing – after all, the number of degrees attained by women in computing fields is only one part of the whole story.

This study is unique in that it investigated the individual microworlds of undergraduate CSE students — the spaces where they experience and begin to appropriate ideas from the computer science domain — to better understand the whole learner and their lived experience not just from an academic perspective, but also from a family, social, and cultural perspective. Some questions that were pursued in this study included why the student decided to major in computer science and whether elements from the *Engagement Practices Framework* are being applied to support their participation in their undergraduate CSE community. This study provides a set of narrow glimpses into the experiences of undergraduate women in a CSE community, however, and is not meant to be representative of the entire sub-culture. The study asked participants to reflect on their community experiences and how they have impacted their desire to pursue a CS major. Therefore, it contributes to a better understanding of the phenomenon of the participation of women in an undergraduate CSE department context. As Sinclair and Kalvala (2015) conclude, in order to develop strategies that will support continued participation by women in undergraduate CS programs, it is essential to understand these students' perspectives as they progress through their CS journey and begin to identify as computer scientists and engineers.

Summary

This chapter examined the existing literature on computer science education to understand why women may not be participating and to look for recommendations for engaging and retaining women in undergraduate CS programs. The body of work presents a range of possible multi-faceted solutions and points to the first undergraduate courses as key intervention points for attracting and retaining members of underrepresented groups, specifically women to the field of computer science.

As described earlier, students have reported perceiving computer science as being boring, antisocial, and irrelevant to their lives. Students also perceive that CS careers are filled with lonely, endlessly detailed work, and the exclusion of under-represented groups. In many novice undergraduate programming courses, women either start behind with less experience, or experience a severe disadvantage when it comes to curriculum, pedagogy, and assessment. These disadvantages can contribute to negative perceptions of the undergraduate CSE environment and of the field in general and are factors that, to different degrees, contribute to students' perceived ability to access a CS identity. The literature reviewed points to the value of rethinking the PreK-12 and undergraduate CS curriculum so that all students are encouraged to identify with CS-related fields.

A review of the literature found no phenomenological studies seeking to understand any of the following: how a sense of belonging is perceived in CSE departments; how inclusivity is perceived in CSE departments; how the newly developed *Engagement Practices Framework*, and other recommended practices from the current literature might contribute to the encouragement, engagement, and retention of women in undergraduate computer science and engineering programs. Chapter three discusses the methods and human subjects concerns for the proposed study.

Chapter Three: Research Methodology

Overview

This study examined the lived experience of female undergraduates in the field of computer science to understand their experiences as women in a major where they are a minority. This chapter presents the research methodology that was used in pursuing the research questions. The research design including its implementation and rationale for choosing a phenomenological, interview-based study as the design for the study are discussed. The selection of participants, as well as the interview techniques that were implemented, data collection techniques, and the method chosen for data analysis, will be discussed. A discussion of issues related to validity and reliability for each relevant step is also included. Institutional Review Board (IRB) considerations will be delineated at the end of this chapter.

Restatement of the Research Questions

This exploratory, phenomenological study investigated the experiences of female undergraduate computer science and engineering students and addresses the following questions:

- What are the lived experiences of female undergraduate computer science and engineering majors?
- What makes undergraduate computer science and engineering departments effective or ineffective spaces for encouraging the participation of female students?
- What types of experiences encourage or discourage participation by a diverse group of female students in undergraduate computer science and engineering departments?

Qualitative Research Design

This qualitative study aimed to explore in detail how participants make sense of their personal lived experiences as women in undergraduate computer science departments. Qualitative research methods are particularly useful for a study seeking to understand a participant's experiences. Concerned with meaning, sense-making, and the subjective experience, qualitative methods allow the researcher and participant to engage in open dialogue, making it less likely that the researcher misinterprets the responses of participants (Storey, 2011). The research design for this exploratory study was phenomenological. It employed qualitative methods to gather data and explore the meaning that participants link to their experiences through semi-structured interviews of undergraduate computer science and engineering majors. A phenomenological study involves exploring how a participant experiences her world and how structures of consciousness construct her world and allow her to perceive it (Gray, 2014). As indicated by Smith (2004), taking a closer look at the particular story of a participant allows us to better understand the universal aspects of a shared humanity. Understanding the experience of a particular person helps us better understand how others might deal with the situation being explored.

Rationale for a phenomenological study. Within qualitative methods, a phenomenological approach is appropriate for understanding the experiences of women as undergraduates in computer science and engineering departments in the United States. Phenomenology can be traced back to philosophers including Kant and Hegel, but Husserl is regarded as the principal founder of phenomenology (Groenewald, 2004). A phenomenological approach supports the gathering of data as a way to form a rich and in-depth understanding of the experiences of participants while allowing for both expected and unexpected meanings to be recognized and drawn out (Moustakas, 1994).

Phenomenology recognizes the authority that a participant has over her own experiences and seeks to understand the world from the point of view of the participant (Gray, 2014). After all, the technical meaning of phenomenology as constructed by Hegel refers to "the science of describing what one perceives, senses, and knows in one's immediate awareness and experience" (Moustakas, 1994, p. 25). Phenomenologists describe the relationship between perception and an object as active, with the human consciousness actively constructing and perceiving the world (Gray, 2014). For this study, it was important to take into consideration the myriad elements that women interact with in undergraduate computer science and engineering environments. Indeed, structures and objects have specific meaning for people who are living, thinking, and experiencing them.

Interpretative phenomenological analysis (IPA). In keeping with a Husserlian phenomenological approach, the aim of this study was to analyze particular cases in order to describe the essence and experience of female undergraduates in the field of computer science and engineering, a major where they are a minority. IPA is appropriate for analysis in this case because it can give insights that correspond with the underlying values and beliefs of the learning environments being studied (Guldberg & Mackness, 2009). IPA recognizes that there are different levels of interpretation that can be drawn through thoughtful analysis (Smith, 2004). The personal experiences of the participants in this study were better understood through the variety of interpretations, afforded by IPA, for the rich verbal accounts recorded in the interviews. The commitment of IPA, then, is to "give voice" to and to "make sense" of the experiences of participants (Larkin, Watts, & Clifton, 2008). Finally, IPA draws from the interpretative or hermeneutic tradition in recognizing the role of the researcher in making sense of the personal experience of each individual (Smith, 2004; Storey, 2011).

Researcher's Role

The role of qualitative research is to be insightful and demonstrate a capacity to understand and the ability to differentiate between what is important and what is not (Gray, 2014). Smith (2004) describes the role of the researcher in IPA as one concerned with making sense of the process by which a participant tries to make sense of their personal and social world. Phenomenological research, then, requires the researcher to reflect upon and acknowledge the interpretative framework that she applies to the data as a way of increasing the transparency of the analysis (Storey, 2011). As Storey (2011) acknowledges, some aspects of the framework applied by the researcher might be unconscious and may not be readily identifiable. For these reasons, it is important to understand the experiences of the researcher in the computer science landscape.

As an undergraduate, the researcher earned a Bachelor of Science degree in Operations and Management Information Systems (OMIS) and a Spanish minor. She was the only woman in several of her computer science classes. As a student-athlete, the researcher benefited from the support of a tutor for most of her programming classes. While the tutor was hired for a male basketball player, she was invited to sit in on all of the tutoring sessions since she was enrolled in the same classes as the male basketball player.

The researcher was active in the OMIS community, serving for over two years as the Service Learning coordinator on the OMIS Student Network. The researcher was awarded the department award for her contributions to the OMIS community. The certificate presented to the researcher read: "for his contributions to the OMIS Community." After college, the researcher completed a yearlong AmeriCorps service placement at an underserved Middle School in San Jose, CA where she taught "computer" class and supported the work of other teachers. The researcher continued to teach Spanish and technology-related classes while earning her California Secondary School Teaching Credential in Spanish and a Master of Arts degree in Interdisciplinary Education with an emphasis in Teaching and Learning with Technology.

The researcher has taught Spanish and computer science at independent schools for over fifteen years. She has also held leadership roles including Computer Science Department Chair and Director of Learning Technologies. She currently serves as the Dean of Studies and teaches two computer science class - Introduction to Computer Science and Intermediate Computer Science - at an all-girls independent school in New York City. The researcher has been involved with computer science education in several ways including as a teacher, member of the Computer Science Teachers Association, member and chairperson of the Pepperdine University student chapter of the Association for Computing Machinery, and as a volunteer teacher in underserved middle schools.

Following the requirements presented by Sokolowski (2000), the researcher will act as a detached observer to the extent to which she can so that she may avoid introducing her bias to the study. The practice of setting aside presuppositions by the researcher was referred to as psychological-phenomenological reduction by Husserl and is also called bracketing (Ashworth, 1999). The purpose of bracketing in phenomenology is to set aside researcher beliefs to allow the "life-world" of the participant in the research to emerge clearly so that it can be studied (Ashworth, 1999).

Sampling Strategy

As recommended by Moustakas (1994), research participants were selected based on their ability to provide comprehensive descriptions of their experiences as women in undergraduate computer science and engineering programs. As suggested by Gray (2014), convenience sampling was employed in order to most easily access subjects for this study. Convenience sampling presents limitations in that it is neither purposeful nor strategic, however it is useful for exploratory research (Gray, 2014). Working from a convenience sample based on the availability of participants leads to a good initial understanding of the experiences of women in undergraduate computer science and engineering programs.

Sampling was oriented to finding the right people who have experience relevant for the study (Flick, 2007). For this study, participants had to identify as female undergraduate students majoring in computer science and engineering. Participants also had to be willing to spend time being interviewed. Additionally, snowball sampling was used to find additional participants. Snowball sampling involved asking interview participants, who have greater knowledge of the field than the researcher, to identify others who would be good to interview (Gray, 2014).

As identified by Smith (2004), the nuanced analysis associated with IPA is only realizable on a small sample size. Therefore, many IPA studies have sample sizes of five to ten (Smith, 2004). The sample size for this study depended on the amount of information necessary in order to present rich descriptions and detailed analysis of the accounts of participants. This initial research project included six participants.

Participation

Female undergraduate computer science and engineering majors who meet the selection criteria were contacted via email and offered an opportunity to participate in the study (see Appendix A). The researcher worked with the computer science and engineering department at a United States West Coast university to identify participants. Participants who agreed to join the study were sent an informed consent form (see Appendix B) describing the purpose of the study as well as the participant's rights and risks in the study. After participants returned a completed informed consent, the researcher gathered initial contact and demographic information from the participant and scheduled an initial interview.

Plan for Data Collection

Qualitative interviews were the main instrument of data collection for this study. As described by Gray (2014), interviews are the favored research technique when the objectives of the researcher are to understand the experiences, opinions, attitudes, values, and processes of the participants; a vast majority of IPA studies have been conducted on data collected from semi-structured interviews (Smith, 2004). The researcher conducted semi-structured interviews and used open-ended questions as a way of allowing for real-time follow up through additional probing questions (Smith, 2004). Through these interviews, study participants were encouraged to share their stories and experiences with the researcher. As a way of encouraging self-interpretation of their lived experience prior to sharing that interpretation and understanding with the researcher, participants were provided context for the interview through an interview guide that included guiding questions (Guldberg & Mackness, 2009). While an interview guide was provided, the interviews were conducted as open-ended and semi-structured. In this type of interview, interesting areas that emerge can be probed through follow-up questions not included in the interview guide.

Interview. Interviews were guided by an interview protocol (see Appendix C) and were conducted remotely using an internet-based conferencing technology called Zoom. Interviews included both voice and video feeds and both were recorded. The interview protocol was designed to facilitate a semi-structured interview process meaning that open-ended questions were used and phrased in accordance with the recommendations presented by Moustakas (1994) and Gray (2014). The interviews addressed "what" and "how" questions (Flick, 2007). While the interviewer had a list of issues and questions to discuss and ask, she did not cover all of them and the order of questions changed for each interview. Furthermore, additional questions were asked based on the direction that each interview took (Gray, 2014). A semi-structured interview approach allows for such probing of views and opinions. Gray (2014) describes the value of semi-structured interviews for exploring and probing the subjective meanings that respondents ascribe to their experiences. It is important to acknowledge that probing during the interview sometimes leads to the diversion of the interview in new directions not originally considered (Gray, 2014).

To be respectful of the participants' time, the interviews were structured as two to four one-hour, remote interviews and were conducted on different days unless the participant requested to complete the full interview in one day. During the interviews, the researcher closely monitored the participants for any discomfort they might have displayed. The interviews began with social conversation as the interviewer was responsible for creating an atmosphere that was relaxed and trusting so the participant felt comfortable responding honestly and comprehensively to the interview questions. Following the opening, participants were asked to describe aspects of their experiences as undergraduate computer science and engineering majors and then reflect on the factors that contributed or could have contributed positively or negatively to their participation in an undergraduate computer science and engineering department. Thus, there was a focus on the participants' experiences first and then the context influencing those experiences.

In order to maintain control of the interview, which was time sensitive, the interviewer had an in-depth understanding of the research objectives of the interview, asked appropriate (planned) questions, and gave appropriate verbal feedback (Gray, 2104, p. 394). The interviewer was responsible for listening carefully to responses and channeling the interview if the respondent began to stray from the intended target. Video and audio interviews were ideal for these distance interviews, and the Zoom video communication platform supported both. In all of the interviews, the researcher found it necessary to verbally probe (in addition to using non-verbal cues) for elaboration on responses or minimize long-winded responses.

The interview protocol helped structure the interview process and allowed for the analysis of the data from a comparative point of view (Flick, 2007). The interview protocol was applied more or less consistently and interviews were similar to one another to allow for a comparison of the interviewees as opposed to having to account for differences in the research situations. In this way, the constant application of the semi-structured interview protocol increased the similarity of the research situation where the data were produced, allowing for the differences in interviewee experiences and attitudes to be drawn. While following the interview protocol facilitated comparison, the key to success for the interview resulted in the ability of the interviewer to improvise when necessary. Some techniques that were applied during the interviews included varying question order, varying the phrasing of the questions in order to help the conversation seem natural, and letting the interview go "off track" to build trust and rapport by raising similar or different experiences (Gray, 2014).

Data Analysis Procedures

One of the challenges of working with qualitative research is making sense of the data and finding coherent meaning in the interview data. Interpretative phenomenological analysis (IPA) is a methodology concerned with understanding the perception of events and experiences by participants. While the aim in many versions of qualitative research is to identify categories or themes for analysis, IPA offers a series of steps to allow the researcher to identify these central categories or themes (Storey, 2011). Drawing on the work advanced by Smith (2004) and Storey (2011), data analysis for the semi-structured interviews in this study followed IPA.

The researcher began the process of data analysis by transcribing the interviews as soon as possible in order to become familiar with the data. The IPA process then continued with the researcher reading and re-reading the transcripts in order to get a general understanding of the tone and flavor of each interview (Storey, 2011). IPA is strongly idiographic; the detailed examination of one case ends when gestalt has been achieved (Smith, 2004). The member check technique was used throughout the interview process to validate the accuracy of the interpretation of the interviews. The researcher then moved on to the second transcript and so on through the corpus of interviews.

Once all interviews were transcribed, the researcher conducted a focused re-reading of the transcripts to identify and make notes on significant responses by participants. The researcher began the coding process by using a priori categories drawn from the literature review in chapter two on the experiences of females in undergraduate computer science and engineering departments and courses. Following the recommendations of Storey (2011), a priori application of theory was used "to inform rather than drive the analysis" (p. 7). The a priori themes were supplemented with emergent themes that arose spontaneously from the interviews. This supports the interrogative characteristic of IPA research and has as a key aim to make a contribution while linking the results of the analysis to existing research (Smith, 2004). The next stage of analysis involved returning to the transcripts and using the notes that were made to produce themes to ensure a clear connection between themes and the data (Storey, 2011). Appendix E shows a list of all of the codes used; the codes that emerged from the interviews are indicated in bold.

At the end of this iterative process, the researcher identified group-level superordinate themes that reflected the core concerns of the interviews and sub-themes that could be illustrated by quotations from the interview transcripts. Table 1 shows the themes used for this study.

Table 1

Theme Definitions

Theme	Definition	Example Quote
Community or Family Exposure	The support or lack of support from close family or friends who participate directly in a CS-related or STEM field before college that contributed to the participant's pursuit of CSE.	"So, my dad's an electrical engineer – my brother is a bioengineer."
Discrimination or Microaggressions	The discrimination or microaggression identified by participants including sexist language, being overpowered by male peers, or otherwise being treated differently as a woman.	"I feel like even the male students can kind of subconsciously judge based on the professor's gender."
Early CS Experiences	The exposure or lack of exposure to CS-related experiences before college including through classmates, teachers, informal education experiences, tinkering independently, etc.	"Our [high school] fabrication lab had laser cutters and 3d printers and stuff like that so I was really into that."
Engagement Practice: Curriculum	The degree to which coursework was described as relevant or irrelevant.	"Overall the class is really interesting just because you're learning about things I'm using everyday like Wi-Fi, Bluetooth, 3G, 4G, stuff like that."
Engagement Practice: Pedagogy	The degree to which course was described as being presented including engaging material, fair grading, humor, mixing lecture and labs, opportunities to apply concepts, etc.	"Having a ton of examples and connecting things to things that like are important in the grand scheme of things so I understand why I am learning it."
Engagement Practice: Recruitment	The exposure participants experienced to their chosen major through recruitment including pre-college and on campus recruitment.	"At orientation, my advisor that was assigned to me he was in the computer engineering department he kind of talked me into it."

(continued)

Theme	Definition	Example Quote
Engagement Practice: Student Academic Support	The academic supports provided or not provided to participants including study groups, on-campus tutoring, availability of professors and TAs, etc.	"I keep going back to the importance of study groups and that's just because, um, not only do you kind of get help from your classmates in terms of questions. But you're hearing questions that you wouldn't have you would have thought about yourself."
Engagement Practice: Student Emotional Support	The emotional supports provided or not provided to participants including student groups, female peer support, mentorships, access to leadership positions, participation in Grace Hopper Celebration, etc.	"I really just started learning about computers, outside just the education but kind of like what computer science is as an industry as well as being a woman in it through ACM-W."
Identity Within CSE	The descriptions participants gave about how they identified as women within the CSE major including disconnection, empowerment, gendered obstacles, etc.	"I did feel like special and kind of empowered but then like I saw that they [male peers] were doing, like, well advanced stuff and I was like I want to be doing that too. Like I want to be getting a good experience out of my internship."
Lessons Learned and Suggestions	The lessons that participants described having learned as part of their experience as undergraduate CSE majors. Participants also offered suggestions for others in the future.	"I think it'd be nice to like hear from a lot of different areas in the field from women and I think it would be like a nice boost for like a reminder of empowerment."
Outside Supports	The outside supports described by students including their involvement in outside communities, the importance of hearing the stories of other females, having most of their friends in other majors, etc. This theme differs from the theme *Community or Family Exposure* because it describes support during the undergraduate experience as opposed to before.	"I think a lot of my support comes from my family. Their support means the most, [more] than like any professors."

(continued)

Theme	Definition	Example Quote
Reasons for Persisting in CS Major	The reasons that participants gave for having persisted in their experiences as undergraduate CSE majors.	"Like I feel more like if I'm helping someone I'm like oh wow that's like so good and then I feel like I want to do it more."
Sense of Belonging	The elements that contributed to participants feeling a sense of belonging as undergraduate CSE majors including seeing female professors teaching, high test scores, and seeing someone like them ahead of them in school or industry.	"I think it's because I enjoyed doing it, I did pretty well ... so I definitely knew I was really interested in engineering,"
Supportive Male Peer Behavior	The behaviors of supportive male peers as described by participants including being aware of language, helpful without being condescending, understanding, including women in their friend group, and ensuring that all were heard.	"I think the best ones aren't the ones who are like yeah women in tech but the ones that like treat me as an equal."

It includes a definition for each and an example from the interviews. By applying the principles of IPA to analyze the interview data, the study parsed the interviews for themes that participants shared, as well as for an understanding of the stories of individual participants (Smith, 2004). Smith (2004) argues that if one case proves particularly rich during the IPA process, conducting a detailed analysis of that single case in order to do it justice is an important area of development for IPA. The researcher remained open to the suggestion by Smith (2004) to consider an in-depth exploration of a single case that might prove particularly compelling among the interviews that were conducted, however the need to focus on one case did not emerge.

Validity and Reliability of the Data Gathering Instruments

The interviews for this study employed techniques to strengthen validity and reliability. The interview protocol included prompts designed to build trust, and prompted participants to expand and illustrate. In addition, the protocol ensured that the length of the interview was appropriate, and contained questions drawn from the literature (Gray, 2014). While conducting the interviews, it was important for the researcher not to influence the answers of the respondents. Phenomenology required that the researcher bracket her assumptions about the phenomenon being studied and act as a detached observer (Sokolowski, 2000). As a way to minimize bias and ensure an accurate account of the interview, factual questions were not altered, probing and prompting were neutral, and interviews were recorded. A semi-structured interview with follow-up questions and minimal casual conversation also minimized researcher bias (Gray, 2014). All interviews were conducted via digital voice and video communication platforms; no interviews were conducted face-to-face. Furthermore, the researcher practiced her interviewing skills through two pilots of the interview protocol. The pilot of the survey instrument was pretested on two female undergraduates not participating in the study prior to being used as a way of ensuring both validity and reliability of the instrument and interview protocol.

It was important that the words of the interviewees be captured accurately (Gray, 2014), which was enabled by conducting them via a digital voice and video communication platform. Possible platforms for the interviews included Skype, Google Hangout, FaceTime, and Zoom. In the end, Zoom was the platform determined to be most accessible for all participants, and both the video and audio feeds were recorded with the participants' permission. By recording both of the audio and video portions of the interviews, the interviewer was able to concentrate on the process of listening and guiding the interview (Gray, 2014). Participant data and interview recordings and notes were stored on a password protected computer with limited access to users other than the interviewer. Storing the interview narrative and notes in this way supporting reliability in the analysis of the interviews and ensures that a peer can access the material for verification and to ensure that proper procedures were followed (Bryman & Bell, 2003).

HyperTRANSCRIBE was used to transcribe the interviews and HyperRESEARCH was used to code the interviews. The use of this software helped the researcher be more consistent and thus better maintain internal validity and reliability. The conversations were transcribed by the researcher to ensure reliability. The member check technique was used to validate the accuracy of the interpretation of the interviews. Member checking was conducted both during the interview process as well as in follow-up conversations, when necessary. Finally, the researcher coded all interviews as part of the iterative process described above to ensure reliability in the application of codes to the data.

Protection of Human Subjects and Ethical Considerations

The risks for human subjects in this study were minimal; the time required for interviews was the biggest imposition. The study procedure required participants to undergo a series of interviews. While there was a time requirement associated with participation, participants were made aware of the time requirements prior to the beginning of the study. The interview focused solely on the experiences of the participant as undergraduate computer science and engineering major. All subjects participated on a volunteer basis, and any potential risks and benefits associated with participating were presented and acknowledged through the Informed Consent Form (see Appendix B). All participants were over the age of eighteen and they were reminded of their right to request not to participate in the study at any point during the interview for any reason.

For the purposes of presenting findings, participants are referred to by a number related to the order of their participation in the first interview. All identifying marks were removed from the data collected. The researcher received approval to conduct this study from the Institutional Review Board (IRB) at Pepperdine University as well as from the IRB at the university where the participants studied.

Participants

The researcher invited study participants through an email sent to female students in two computer science degree programs at one university. Women who were juniors and seniors enrolled in a computer science degree program in either the school of Arts and Sciences or in the School of Engineering were invited to participate. Two students responded to the initial email invitation to participate. Through snowball sampling, a total of six students agreed to participate in the study. Participants completed two one-hour long interviews or one two-hour interview. Interviews were recorded using the video conference tool Zoom.us. All participants agreed to participate in follow-up interview and email conversations for further member checking and to validate the accuracy of the understanding of the researcher.

In the end, all of the study participants were enrolled in the School of Engineering and were pursuing a Bachelor of Science in Computer Science and Engineering. The participants reported very few women in their major. In the senior class, there were seven women total and four of them participated in this study. The total number of students enrolled in the major in each year was reported to be between 70 – 80. While statistics for the specific Computer Science and Engineering department were not made available to the researcher, enrollment percentages by gender for the 2016-17 school year for the School of Engineering as a whole were published. There were 28% women enrolled among the six majors in the School of Engineering including: Bioengineering, Civil Engineering, Computer Science and Engineering, Electrical Engineering, Mechanical Engineering, and Web Design and Engineering.

Demographics. Table 2 describes the participants' age, year in school, self-identified race, and level of prior computer science experience.

Table 2

Demographics for Participants in Order of First Interview

Participant	Nickname	Age	Year in School	Race	Prior CS Experience
Participant 1	Whitehat	22	Senior	Asian Indian	None
Participant 2	Robotics	21	Junior	Native-Hawaiian	Informal: Ruby
Participant 3	Dorm Sister	22	Senior	Black	None
Participant 4	Theta Tau	21	Junior	Japanese	None
Participant 5	Technovation	22	Senior	Chinese and Vietnamese	Informal: Technovation
Participant 6	Positive Googler	22	Senior	Asian	AP Computer Science

All study participants were 21 or 22-year-old females. Two participants were Juniors and four were Seniors in college. They came from diverse racial and socioeconomic backgrounds. One of the participants identified as Black, one identified as Indian, one identified as Chinese and Vietnamese, one as Japanese, one as Native-Hawaiian, and one as Asian. There were no Latina or White participants. Two of the six participants had a family member or friend in computer engineering. All of the other participants knew someone, a family friend or teacher, in another STEM field. One of the six participants came to her college experience knowing that she wanted to study computer science and engineering; she had taken a programming class – AP Computer Science A – in high school. The five other participants did not have any formal programming experience and declared computer science and engineering as their major during the freshman year in college. Data saturation was identified by the lack of new themes emerging from the interviews.

Participant Descriptions

Participant 1. Participant 1 is nicknamed White Hat in this study because of her interest in information security. She identified as Indian American and described a very close relationship with her family. Her mother had a high school education and works as a social worker. Her father is a mechanical engineer who dropped out of school in 5th or 6th grade. He owns an auto repair shop in the U.S. White Hat described her sister as "the only person in my family that's gone to college." White Hat had a difficult time adjusting to college and lost all of her freshman year friends outside the major. White Hat had an internship that started freshman year and she kept it all four years. She was a leader in ACM-W and really brought together the group of 7 senior women in the CSE department. This participant had many interests outside of school and enjoyed pursuing side projects not related to technology like blogging about healthy beauty products. She described enjoying ethics and philosophy courses as well, and hoped to continue working in trustworthy computing and information security.

Participant 2. Participant 2, a junior, is nicknamed Robotics because of her interest and active participation in robotics at the university. Both of her parents are optometrists and they encouraged her to go into a field other than optometry or healthcare. She described her high school as very STEM-focused. Students had access to a fabrication lab and Robotics described enjoying the time she spent there. In college, she described spending most of her time in the robotics lab and was very interested in the hardware side of CSE. Robotics had a mix of male and female friends and she described some problems where the junior year women were unsupportive to one another. She realized an interest in electrical engineering after her first year and wants to work on power grids and sustainable energy.

Participant 3. Participant 2 is nicknamed Dorm Sister, a senior, because of her work as a "dorm sister" at her university during summer computer science camps and her interest in sharing the major with other young women. While she was born in the U.S., her parents immigrated from Northern Africa. She did not say what her parents did, but described having aunts and uncles who were electrical engineers. This participant described only having female friends for religious reasons. In addition, she connected with an outside mentor during a panel discussion hosted on her campus and communicates regularly over email with this mentor who is working in Dorm Sister's dream job as a NASA engineer. Dorm Sister described wanting to pursue computer science and engineering because she I knew that she could create something for society and she was attracted to that idea.

Participant 4. Participant 4 is nicknamed Theta Tau because of her founding role and active participation in the Theta Tau honors society. She described her parents as both being technologically savvy; they had both worked for Sony. Theta Tau did not mention the education her mother received, however, her father majored in electrical engineering. She was the second junior interviewed and she was very active in the integration of STEM student groups on campus. She also brought together a group of students to discuss the needs for a new Engineering building that was in the building stages when she found out that there had been no consultation with students during the design process. Theta Tau, like the other junior year participant had mostly male friends in the major. She was also very involved with outside interests and groups and had a leadership role in the Hawaii cultural club on campus. Theta Tau was very interested in becoming immersed in the engineering field in her early career and eventually moving into a management role.

Participant 5. Participant 5, a senior, is nicknamed Technovation because that is the program that she participated as a high school student that connected her to her near-peer mentor, a young woman who attended the university where she would enroll (the university where this study occurred). She described her parents as immigrants and her mother works as a registered nurse and her father as a pastor. Technovation described pursuing the CSE degree because it was the most interesting to her of all of the engineering offerings. While she described struggling through her major, her near-peer mentor and one female faculty mentor were essential in helping her persist.

Participant 6. Participant 6 was nicknamed Positive Googler because she described the interview process as a walk down memory lane. She had just completed her senior year, graduated, and she had just lined up a job at Google. Her mother was a health coach, her father was an engineer at a large semiconductor company and always encouraged her to tinker with technology. This played a large role in her pursuit of the field. Her older brother was a bioengineer and she described that she and her brother always had access to STEM activities and resources. She also described spending large amounts of time dancing, she double majored in dance and CSE. Positive Googler described her relief at realizing that she did not have to code in her free time to end up in a job like the one she was going to start. She was excited to bring together her passion for dance and CS in order to expose other young women to the field.

Summary

This chapter summarizes the methodology for this study of the lived experience of female undergraduates in the field of computer science and engineering. An exploratory phenomenological design was used for this study and analysis followed an interpretive phenomenological approach. Semi-structured interviews were used to gather information on the experiences of participants and how they make sense of that personal experience. The data was analyzed by the researcher using coding methods consistent with IPA. Internal validity and reliability were maintained through the study design. Finally, IRB and Human Subjects considerations were addressed. In chapter four, the results of this study are presented.

Chapter Four: Results

This chapter describes the results of this phenomenological study on the lived experience of young women in undergraduate computer science and engineering programs. Specifically, this study incorporated an interpretative phenomenological analysis (IPA) in seeking to understand the perception of events and experiences by participants. IPA involves a series of steps to allow the researcher to identify these central categories or themes in the research. The process began with the transcription of the interviews soon after they were conducted. The transcriptions were read and re-read, they were also member-checked by participants. Interviews were coded using a priori categories drawn from the literature review and the a priori themes were supplemented with emergent themes that arose spontaneously from the interviews. The research questions are restated and addressed below with the participants words included to illuminate the topics in question. A summary of the themes that emerged from the study concludes this chapter.

Restatement of the Research Questions

This exploratory study investigates the experiences of female undergraduate computer science and engineering students and addresses the following questions:

- What are the lived experiences of female undergraduate computer science and engineering majors?
- What makes undergraduate computer science and engineering departments effective or ineffective spaces for encouraging the participation of female students?
- What types of experiences encourage or discourage participation by a diverse group of female students in undergraduate computer science and engineering departments?

Modifications Based on Pilot Interviews

Two pilot interviews were conducted with recent graduates from undergraduate computer science programs. Based on the pilot interviews, modifications were made to the interview protocol (See Appendix C). As a result of receiving zero responses for participation from the initial email invitation, the researcher consulted with the dissertation chairperson and decided to offer compensation of a $25 Starbucks or Amazon gift card. The IRB committees were notified of the change and an updated IRB protocol was submitted and approved.

Answers to the Research Questions

Answers to each research question are considered in the sections below. Note that questions 2 and 3 are each separated into two parts each since there is a dichotomy between what makes the department effective or ineffective as well as between the experiences that encourage and discourage participation.

What are the lived experiences of female undergraduate computer science and engineering majors? Key experiences described by the participants about their experiences as computer science and engineering majors are summarized in themes in Table 3.

Table 3

Key Experiences for Women in a Computer Engineering Undergraduate Program

Key Experience	Participants Who Described It (Out of 6 Total)	Times Occurred
Felt Included	6	27
Imposter Behavior and Thoughts	6	25
Early Experience: Did Not Know What CS World Was Like	5	18
Positive Experience Overall	6	17
Aware of Low Female Participation	5	17
Bonded with other Women in CSE	4	10
Collaborative Environment	4	10
Saw Someone Like Her in Industry or School	4	10
Early Experience: Did Well in STEM Courses	5	8
Felt Disconnected	4	7
Felt Empowered	3	7
Needed Help to Recognize Discrimination	3	7
Felt Unprepared for CSE Courses	5	6
Felt Alone in the Major	4	6
Most College Friends Not in Major	4	6
Did Not See Self Reflected in CS World	4	5
Did Not Find Most Negative Stereotypes to be True	1	1
Felt Prepared for CSE Courses	0	0

Note. The table was sorted based on times occurred.

All of the participants reported a positive experience overall in their undergraduate computer science and engineering major and described feeling included 27 times across all six interviews, the most frequently occurring theme. All six participants also described having experienced imposter behavior and thoughts 25 times across all six interviews; this was almost as frequently as they described feeling included. Five of the six participants came to the major with limited knowledge about the computer science and engineering world. None of the participants felt prepared for their CSE courses. Participants described not knowing what the formal education world was like nor what the industry options were for them. All of the participants reported staying in the major because felt like they had good friends to support their progress.

What makes undergraduate computer science and engineering departments effective spaces for encouraging the participation of female students? All of the young women interviewed described learning more about their role as young women within the field of computer engineering. Factors that make undergraduate computer science and engineering departments effective spaces for encouraging the participation of female students are shown in Table 4.

Table 4

Factors that Make Undergraduate Computer Science Departments Effective Spaces for Encouraging the Participation of Female Students

Factor	Participants Who Described It (Out of 6 Total)	Times Occurred
Female Professors Mentoring and Creating Inclusive Environments	6	23
Value of Community and Networking	6	19
Available Professors	6	17
Female Peer Support: Emotional	6	15
Additional Supports for Women	6	14
Participation in Grace Hopper Celebration	6	14
Leadership Positions or Participation in CS-related Club	5	10
Saw Someone Like Her in Industry or School	5	10

(continued)

Factor	Participants Who Described It (Out of 6 Total)	Times Occurred
Collaborative Environment	4	10
Male Peer Support: Emotional	3	8
Male Professors Mentoring and Creating Inclusive Environments	3	6
Hearing Another Female's Story	4	4
Confidence Seeing Female Professors	3	4
Mentoring Younger Women	2	2

Note. The table was sorted based on times occurred.

All six participants described the valuable experience of traveling to the Grace Hopper Celebration for Women in Computing (GHC) and spending time with successful female engineers. The students described that all of the women in their major had an open invitation to travel to GHC. They simply had to respond to a participation email and they were enrolled in the conference. All expenses were paid for by the school. One student described this experience as eye-opening for her because it allowed her to see people who were more like her. She said:

> I feel like I was able to see more women who were just like regular people, and I was like 'yes!' because I thought I had to like you know build my own computer and like have to do all like these modifications to my computer [to be an engineer]. I'm not that kind of person, but like a lot of the people I talked to at Grace Hopper there were more like normal or like regular just like you know people who don't modify all their computers and it was nice to see that that didn't have to be the case to like get a good job. (Participant Robotics)

All of the participants described a deeper understanding of the specific issues women face in the field as a result of their participation in the GHC. Describing her GHC experience, one participant said:

> Just to see how great women are in the computer science industry. I've seen women from all over the world from all different kinds of backgrounds being leaders in the computer science industry and even like very high positions like CFOs and CEOs. So that's really cool! It's been very helpful I think that's honestly one of the reasons I have

been able to be, I think, pretty successful in the school of engineering. Having that additional support and kind of that support kind of giving me the motivation to kind of step out of my comfort zone and kind of do more. (Participant Dorm Sister)

Another student described GHC as being essential in helping her see women in the fields of computer science and engineering. She described:

No, I didn't know about anyone in the field at all like, no. Now I know about like Grace Hopper and stuff but like before it was just some field and it seemed like it was just men at computers. (Participant Technovation)

For another participant, GHC opened up her eyes to some of the issues for women in computing and it also provided a resource for her as she turned to her job search.

It was just inspiring to see like oh it's like a celebration for women in computing they had a lot of like inspiring talks and the keynote speaker was really good and I think it's just the positive energy of having all these women in tech. A lot of the sessions were really cool, especially hearing people in industry and their personal experiences and like how a lot of it is difficult but they're able to like work through a lot of it. It's just reassuring. Obviously, like a big problem in tech fields is that women will like join but then they won't necessarily stay in these roles. Right, so that was like really interesting to me because obviously I didn't know that there were like no women in [computer engineering]. I knew like engineering in general tended to be male-dominated I didn't know that to take engineering and then computer engineering is literally like way less. The main reason that I'm returning to Grace Hopper is that they sort of have like an enormous career fair. (Participant Theta Tau)

Yet another participant (Robotics) described GHC as a place where she was able to find people who are "not as much of your stereotypical computer engineers. I just feel like they're easier to get along with." She continued her description of her experience at GCH this way:

> I feel like every woman in computing should go because I just feel like it's an empowering conference, you know? I feel like I don't remember if I was like doubting myself then, but I feel like when I went to Grace Hopper I was like very much like oh I'm a computer engineer, this is the best! You know, I feel like I didn't have any doubts. Yeah, I really enjoyed it. (Participant Robotics)

One participant, Technovation, described the importance of being "a proud feminist" and said this about returning to GHC once she was in industry: "I think it would be like a nice boost for like a reminder of empowerment."

Three participants described male professors creating inclusive environments and encouraging their participation. All six students described female professors or mentors creating inclusive environments and encouraging them. One student described a female professor creating an inclusive learning experience that encouraged her participation this way:

> Yeah, [Female Mentor], um she's in the computer engineering department and she's been like super helpful because like I feel like she's always really encouraging even like, I don't know, not that our tests were like easy, but I felt like I understood the way like computer engineering like worked and then I was like oh. And then when I would take her test like it was really good and she'd always be like oh good job, you know.
>
> (Participant Robotics)

In addition to GHC, all of the participants described additional supports that were available to them as young women in the department including the women in engineering luncheons, events put on by the department, the support of the female faculty members, and female peers support, and most described their participation in the women's chapter of ACM. One student said this about those additional supports:

> It's been very helpful. I think that's honestly one of the reasons I have been able to be, I think, pretty successful in the school of engineering. Having that additional support and

kind of that support kind of giving me the motivation to kind of step out of my comfort zone and kind of do more. (Participant Dorm Sister)

Another student acknowledged that the extra supports she received as a female were nice, but she felt that she would have persisted and been successful in the major even if those supports had not been made available to her. She said:

Yeah, it's not like I mean like yeah there's been people who are like encouraging and stuff, but it's not like I don't think they're the reason why I stayed. It's just more me like not wanting to quit. Like because yeah even if those things didn't happen I think I'd still be here. (Participant Robotics)

Three students also described feeling an increase in confidence seeing female professors teaching their classes. They reported that seeing themselves reflected in the faculty and a relatively even distribution of male to female faculty in the department. Participants did not know with certainty what the faculty gender distribution looked like during the 2016-17 school year and the school does not publish those statistics, but one participant shared that when she started she was happy to see a good number of women on the faculty in her department. She said:

I want to say almost half of our professors are female which is really, really nice for us few ladies here to actually kind of get somehow additional support. It kind of gives you some sense of confidence to see another woman up there teaching the course. (Participant Dorm Sister)

All six participants also described either a formal or informal mentor relationship with one particular female professor; the professor is referred to above as well and here as "Female Mentor." Five of the six women recounted speaking with her regardless of whether or not she was their designated advisor. Robotics described having her as her teacher in her first computer engineering course and then choose her as their advisor. Dorm Sister stated: "And also, my advisor [Female Mentor] has just been a tremendous help."

Another described her situation like this; she had not had this female professor as an advisor nor was she her advisor:

> I think a big influence in sort of helping me keep confidence was [Female Mentor] that professor I mentioned before, yeah, I've actually never taken her class before but yeah. I just think she's really cool so the first…a few times I just emailed her and asked if I could go in and talk to her and she's always had her door open and really was open to talking with me. And especially, like my sophomore and junior years, and then leading into this year she's been super supportive and every time I go talk to her now. She told me I should go get a PhD. But yeah like I've been in her office so many times especially looking for internships and jobs and when everyone else already had theirs. I was like [Female Mentor], does no one care about my GPA, does no one care that I want a job. She was like [name] there's a job for everyone, like, you can do it; you're really smart. (Participant Positive Googler)

The same participant later described this professor this way:

> One of our professors [Female Mentor], she really heads sort of bringing together the female community. Every finals week, she would host a woman in computing lunch and bring us free food while we were studying and that was a great way for me to meet upperclassmen especially when I was younger. I felt part of that community so it was really cool, like right off the bat. (Participant Positive Googler)

Another participant felt supported by this same professor who encouraged her to declare computer engineering as her major:

> And then I'd go talk to her and she'd be just like you should definitely you know like declare a major in this field, and I was like oh that's a good idea you know like, she was

always like helping me do things like was giving advice, and like sending me emails saying like oh there's this thing you guys should go to. (Participant Robotics)

This same student described this professor as someone who created an inclusive learning environment for her just by being available. She said: "Yeah [Female Mentor], again just because she's so nice, she's easy going and like I know she's really easy to open up to and she really cares." Another participant described the finals week luncheon that this professor organized:

> It was a chance to come together for free lunch like then like girls could share their experiences talk about the quarter and I think that going to those made me aware that there are clubs that I could be part of and clubs that I could use as a resource and so I don't know, like I know that's like a really random thing but every quarter, those lunches, I looked forward to and like I just knew that most of the girls could find time out of their week to just hang out. (Participant Technovation)

All students described the full-time faculty in their school as being available to them and approachable during office hours or by appointment. An exception was noted for adjunct professors who were described as being less accessible than full-time faculty members. One participant described the supportive female faculty members this way:

> Overall, I think the faculty, the female faculty, are really supportive and are really kind of working hard to kind of cater an environment that's very inclusive to women and kind of finding different ways to empower them um so I think that's just something I really like about our School of Engineering. (Participant Dorm Sister)

Two students described having positive relationships overall with a male professor or advisor. All students described having at least one friend that they could turn to for help in each of their classes. One student described turning to mostly males for help because there were more males than females in her classes. Theta Tau said: "I'm going to reach out to someone who's like taking the class at the same time as me or is in the same class as me but yeah obviously, it's usually guys." The young women described the behavior of supportive male peers which included treating women equally, being aware of their language, and being helpful without being condescending. More of this supportive behavior will be described below in the section that summarizes the themes from the research.

All participants described a unique bond with their female classmates. In addition to the close bond with the other women, participants also described an assumed confidentiality among the women. They felt comfortable sharing their experiences, including issues that came up, with one another. Besides classes, one way that participants connected with other women in their department was through department-sponsored clubs and events.

The six participants interviewed had all participated in club meetings, and five of the six participated regularly with at least one club. The clubs included Association of Computing Machinery (ACM), Association of Computing Machinery Women's Chapter (ACM-W), Society of Black Engineers (SBE), Society of Women Engineers (SWE), and Theta Tau, the professional engineering fraternity. Overall, the clubs were described as important for spaces for encouraging their participation.

As one participant indicated:

There was a lot of opportunities in terms of like my club [ACM-W] I've been an officer since my freshman year secretary my freshman and sophomore year and then I was vice president my junior year and then now I'm a co-president this year. I like that the department gives us a lot of funding so we can put on a bunch of events. (Participant White Hat)

Another participant described the department-sponsored groups available to her as a woman as essential in helping her cope with some of the things that came up for her in her experience as a young woman in the department. The student described conversations within these groups as confidential. She said:

> [In] groups like Society of Women Engineers and Association of Computing Machinery Women's chapter, um, I don't know, we just talk about our experiences together about being female students in engineering. I was surprised that I was…they were pretty much going through the same thing I was and I just wasn't expecting that. (Participant Dorm Sister)

Engagement Practice: Grow Positive Student Community. As described above, all of the participants described being grateful for the additional supports for women that were available in their department. All of the participants also described the availability of professors, the support of female professors, and study groups as contributing to a positive learning community. Leadership positions and participation in CS-related clubs and a collaborative environment also contributed positively for these students. One participant described her experience this way:

> Being in the major, all of my classes I felt really comfortable and I like how the environment that we have in our classrooms is really collaborative and really friendly, and... I've made all of my closest friends in the department and I don't feel like we're ever competing against one another. Which, I've talked to friends at like other schools and sometimes environments can be different than that. (Participant Positive Googler)

Engagement Practice: Build Student Confidence and Professional Identity. Participants described not knowing what the formal education world was like nor what the industry options were for them when they started their undergraduate experiences. As described above, all of the participants benefited from participating in the Grace Hopper Celebration, which was described as an opportunity to develop a professional identity and a sense of belonging. Participants also benefited from hearing other females' stories as well as from seeing someone ahead of them in industry or in school. Participants also described their relationships with their female professors and their female peers as experiences that build their confidence.

What makes undergraduate computer science and engineering departments ineffective spaces for encouraging the participation of female students? Table 5 describes the factors that make undergraduate computer science and engineering departments ineffective spaces for encouraging the participation of female students.

Table 5

Factors that Make Undergraduate Computer Science Departments Ineffective Spaces for Encouraging the Participation of Female Students

Factor	Participants Who Described It (Out of 6 Total)	Times Occurred
Condescending Male Peer	5	10
Sexist Language	3	10
Treated Differently as Woman	3	8
Discrimination/Microaggression Towards Female Professor	3	7
Male-centered Language	3	5
Pressure to Conform to Male-Centered Environment	2	2
Affirmative Action Attribution	1	2

Note. The table was sorted based on times occurred.

All participants in the study described the low number of females as something that they noticed. One participant acknowledged often being the only female in a class or in a lab. White Hat said: "you'd be the only girl in your class or in your lab. That's happened to me a lot of times." Positive Googler described always counting how many girls there were in the class and finding it "funny."

Another student described that it was different to work with mostly males. She did not feel like she was able to share some of her interests with her male friends. She described it this way:

> So, it's just like slightly different...I can't be like oh my gosh like Aero Pos[tal] is having a sale or you know like there's like a sale at like Forever 21 or something like no one cares. So yeah you know I mean like it's just like it's like small things. (Participant Robotics)

She went on to say: "When I was hanging out with a lot of my engineering friends and they were all guys, I was like okay I think I need to like not just hang out with guys."

Participants described computer science world stereotypes and not thinking they fit in. White Hat said that she did not feel included by some of her male peers. She said: "a lot of the guys didn't want to work with the girl students." This participant also had this to say about the male students: "They thought that [the female students] were, I don't know, maybe not as smart." While all of the students saw evidence of these stereotypes in their undergraduate experience, one student described being appreciative that she didn't find all of the negative stereotypes that she had been warned about to be accurate.

Three students described inappropriate conduct and sexist language from male professors in general. Two students spoke about the same professor. Dorm Sister put it this way: "Also kind of just some things some of the male professors, what they say is kind of sexist." Sexist language used in class by a male professor was reported by three of the six participants. One young woman described a male professor who was teaching a mostly-male class making a sexist comment about a young woman who accidentally walked into his class on the first day of school. Of all of the instances that were described where a male professor conducted himself inappropriately or used sexist language only one time did someone speak up and tell the professor that that was inappropriate and that person was a female who was a senior at the time. Students did describe an anonymous reporting tool that they were made aware of during 2016-2017 school year that they could use to report inappropriate behavior by people on campus. Technovation described this tool this way: "I didn't find out about it until this year. I wish I had known about it a lot longer, but it's something that's available."

One student described feeling discriminated against by a female professor. She described the situation this way:

> I'm not talking about like male professors like a female professor was like I don't think that you should be a president of a club during your senior year, you won't be able to

handle the workload but she didn't say that to the guy [club leader] person. (Participant White Hat)

Three participants reported having witnessed at least one instance of a microaggression directed toward their female professors by their male peers. One case was described by two different participants, and it involved male students questioning a female professor and actively trying to get her fired. Participants reported that this professor left at the end of the term. One participant gave this description of the situation:

> So, I feel like a lot of my male classmates will also look down on the female professors in our department. I hardly hear them complaining so much about the male professors as they do the female professors. There was one that they would really, like, discredit her and talk back in class and they even had like a group chat titled like fire professor blah blah blah. And they submitted so many complaints about her and really like she wasn't that bad. And me and my female classmates couldn't help but feel like it's just because she was a woman. Yeah, they were always complaining about her and they sent so many complaints and they sent it to the Dean and then that year she happened to leave. I mean, she had been teaching there for like longer than we had been there so yeah. I didn't think she was that bad, so yeah, I feel like even the male students can kind of subconsciously judge based on the professor's gender. (Participant Technovation)

One participant reported feeling like the women's chapter of ACM was discouraging and embarrassing because she didn't think that it was well organized and she did not see it as a resource for her. Another young woman who had a leadership position in this group also discussed conflict within the officer group. She described the conflict among the officers as "petty" and had this to say about it:

> For how much effort I put into this club they're still very catty women. A lot of just like disrespect I'd say. I've noticed that the younger officers some of them are really mean-spirited. I'd never had to like reprimand women like around my same around my same

age for being mean. I literally had to sit down with two of my officers and I was like if I see this behavior continue on there's no place for you on my officer team. (Participant White Hat)

What types of experiences encourage participation by a diverse group of female students in undergraduate computer science and engineering departments? Table 6 describes the types of experiences that encourage participation by a diverse group of female students in undergraduate computer science and engineering departments.

Table 6

Types of Experiences that Encourage Participation by a Diverse Group of Female Students in Undergraduate Computer Science Departments

Experience	Participants Who Described It (Out of 6 Total)	Times Occurred
Interest	6	20
Broad Content Area	6	14
Study Groups	6	14
Male Peer Support: Academic	5	13
Relevant and Interesting Assignments	5	12
Practice	5	11
Female Peer Support: Academic	6	10
Engaging Material	4	10
Supportive TA	4	10
Professors Who Engage Students	5	9
Opportunities to Apply Concepts	4	9
Passion for Subject: Professors	4	8
Relevant Coursework	3	7
On-campus Tutoring	2	6
Mixing Lecture with Lab	3	5
Office Hours	3	5
Writing Code Out on the Board	3	5
Professors Who Check of Understanding	3	4
Pair Programming	2	2
Fair Grading	1	1

Note. The table was sorted based on times occurred.

All students reported being very interested in their major and finding it both interesting and satisfying even when they struggled with it. Three of the participants described the content area as difficult and also described a stressful situation that came up when trying to grasp a concept in class or in lab. Even so, all three of those participants said that their experience with difficulty was expected and that they got through it. Dorm Sister described a moment when things just "clicked" for her. She said: "it kind of just clicked at some point and started making sense and I really started enjoying it but before then I really did not know anything."

The participants in this study described their deep interest for the topics in their field as what helped them keep going in their majors. Participants also described a particular engagement when they were given relevant and interesting assignments in their classes. All six students cited the nuances within the field and the broad content area and application as reasons for their persistence in and continued curiosity about computer engineering. Participants reported a continued affinity in their major because, as Theta Tau stated: "For me you can never like stop learning in this field. Especially since it's always changing and growing which I find really interesting."

All six participants reported working with study groups and also found them to be valuable learning experiences. One participant described the sociocultural value of her study groups this way:

> It became a lot easier to do well in them because I was able to kind of get that additional support from my classmates. I keep going back to the importance of study groups and that's just because not only do you kind of get help from your classmates in terms of questions. But you're hearing questions that you would have never thought about yourself and sort of bringing a whole other level to that studying and taking it a step further. So, my computer science classes, doing well in them became a lot easier later on when I did get to know my classmates a lot more. (Participant Dorm Sister)

Four participants described working with at least one supportive teaching assistant (TA). One student described her experience with a particularly supportive TA this way:

There was one TA that stood out. He wasn't like biased towards any student. Like it didn't matter their race or their genders. Like he would just sit down and teach you what you needed to. I really valued that. (Participant White Hat)

One student described the importance of fair and equal grading. When it was fair and equal it was encouraging. Grading will also be discussed in the context of experiences that discourage participation in the next section.

Engagement Practice: Make the Content Matter. Participants acknowledged that professors matter just as much as content. Dorm Sister described a class she enjoyed this way: "I think I liked the professor and the content so I really enjoyed that class overall." One student described the courses where she enjoyed the content as ones where retaining what she learned was not as challenging. She said:

I think those classes I really loved because they were more sort of applicable to things you know and I guess to me in the real world that I think are really interesting. All my other classes, I feel like were just me learning things that I needed to learn, yeah. And I feel like it wasn't until Junior and Senior year that I got super excited about what I was learning [and] I could keep that information [in my mind]. (Participant Positive Googler)

This student went on to describe what classes and professors stood out to her and she said:

I think that's what stands out the most. So, they usually had humor involved, they were fair, and where you can tell when a professor is super excited to teach what they're about to teach. I think that makes a big difference in me being interested in what they're trying to teach me. (Participant Positive Googler)

Participants also described the value of opportunities to apply concepts through practice, labs, and relevant and interesting assignments.

What types of experiences discourage participation by a diverse group of female students in undergraduate computer science and engineering departments? Table 7 describes the types of experiences that discourage participation by a diverse group of female students in undergraduate computer science and engineering departments.

Table 7

Types of Experiences that Discourage Participation by a Diverse Group of Female Students in Undergraduate Computer Science Departments

Experience	Participants Who Described It (Out of 6 Total)	Times Occurred
Unsupportive Male Peer	2	5
Menial Tasks Assigned	3	4
Unsupportive TA	3	4
Overpowered by Male Peers	3	3
Not Invited to Study Groups	2	3
Unsupportive Female Peer	2	3
Answers in Class Double-checked by Male Peers (didn't happen to male peers)	2	2
Females Graded More Easily by Male Professor	1	1

Note. The table was sorted based on times occurred.

Participants reported having unsupportive male peers as well as unsupportive TAs. One participant described an unsupportive comment from a male peer about her grade in a class.

I always arrived like pretty early and [Male Professor] he'd be talking to me a lot and then...I wasn't aware of like anything weird. But then, I had my male friend say like oh you probably like a good grade cuz you were always flirting with him in class. And I was like why would I flirt with someone who's, like, so creepy? Like I'm just like being like a friendly student like responding back to the professor. (Participant Technovation)

Two participants described unsupportive male peer behavior in the form of having their answers in class or in lab questioned. One of them described it this way:

Sometimes when a guy like asked [a female student] a question from homework like they would always have to confirm with another male before like it's... believing the answer. (Participant Positive Googler)

Another echoed the same idea:

> Yeah like if I say something they like have to like double check it and I'm just like where do you think I got my information like. Like you're wasting time. (Participant White Hat)

She described having to first prove her strength as a CS student before being invited to join a study group. She described microaggressions from her male peers this way:

> I noticed that like when you did well and a guy would see that then they would say, oh, she's smart maybe we should invite her to our study groups. But if they thought you weren't smart you would be... not invited to like anything. They would look at you weird if you ask them a question stuff like that. (Participant White Hat)

Students also described their male peers as well as female and male professors as reinforcing stereotypes about the low number of women in computer engineering. One student described this situation:

> People that sort of reinforce the stereotype is really frustrating to me. I guess yeah like when other guys just sort of comment on like make jokes about how many females are in engineering in general. I don't know it's like, can you not, sort of thing. (Participant Theta Tau)

Recommendations for encouraging participation.

One participant reported wishing that male peers thought before speaking. When responding to the question: Do you have any recommendations for male peers who want to be supportive of the women in your major? she said:

> The way you talk can be...they just kind need to be aware of what they're saying. (Participant Dorm Sister)

She went on to say:

> I mean there's always going to be a few guys who think they're better or whatnot but there's definitely a good group of guys who support us just as well as the women. (Participant Dorm Sister)

One participant described being graded differently as a female. One male professor gave her more points for the same answer that her male peer had gotten fewer points for. Participants described their favorite professors as the ones who were fair, brought a sense of humor, and made it clear that they really enjoyed the material they were teaching.

One participant described wishing that their professors had created more inclusive environments. Several participants described wishing their professors made more of an effort to make sure that the young women were heard and encouraged to participate more in their classes. One student shared her recommendation this way:

> So just making I guess a more inclusive environment as well as really encouraging the women in the classroom to participate as much as the males. Creating a very inclusive environment, less of like a bro environment. (Participant Dorm Sister)

White Hat described an interaction with her TA in a lab where she asked for feedback on her code and his response included an expletive. She said:

> Okay, so I was about to run my code and I was like any last tips before I like run this because it would take a really long time to for it to go through. So, he said don't f**k it up. (Participant White Hat)

The participant pushed back on his response, and this is how she described that interaction:

> He was all like I'm teaching you this now because in industry no one's going to hold your hand. And I'm like I'm sorry that you face that. In my industry, I go through training. Just because that's the reality for you doesn't mean it's a reality for me. He was at a loss of words that I like stood up for myself. (Participant White Hat)

Lessons learned and advice for young women just starting in the major. Table 8 describes some of the recommendations that the participants had for young women beginning their journeys in undergraduate computer science and engineering departments.

Table 8

Recommendations for Young Women Pursuing Computer Science and Engineering

Recommendation	Number of Participants Who Described It (Out of 6 Total)	Times Occurred
Value of Community and Networking	6	19
Study Groups	6	14
Practice	5	11
Use On-campus Tutoring	2	6
Don't be Afraid to Fail	4	5
Participation in Grace Hopper Celebration	4	5
Reach out When You are Struggling	4	5
Grades are Important but not that Important	2	4
Side Projects are Important	2	4
A Variety of Paths to Get to Careers in the Field	3	3
Don't Compare Yourself to Others	2	3
Speak Up for Yourself	2	3
Internships are Available at All Levels	2	2
Embracing Feminism	1	1
Value of Mentor in Industry	1	1

Note. The table was sorted based on times occurred.

Participants had a variety of recommendations for young women just staring in the major. Two students described not comparing themselves to others in the major and going at their own pace as advice they wished they had gotten when they had started as undergraduates. One student described it like this:

> I was always just comparing myself to them and like oh I'll never be as smart as them because they've had all this exposure early on. Or, like oh they already have like internships at big companies. But slowly, I realized they're all individuals going out there and I'm just an individual going out there in the space. So being able to move myself [away] from that comparison, I was able to justify myself and know my path is going to be different and it's okay if like I'm not at the same level. Um yeah, that was a big lesson for me. (Participant Technovation)

Five of the six participants emphasized the importance of practicing programming. One participant described what she learned about the value of practicing this way:

> I think...someone said one time like computer science it's something that you have to practice. If you're in engineering you have to practice. It's not like you have it or you don't. It's kind of like practicing piano. But I think that that really impacted me a lot because it kind of really like pushed it into my head that you can't only do this in school. To be successful you should take on a side project or you should, you know, spend some more time outside of school doing it. (Participant Positive Googler)

This same young woman described a mutually beneficial relationship with one of her male peers. They had both taken AP Computer Science in high school and started the introductory series together after their fellow majors had taken two classes together; they had bonded immediately. From that first class on, they took almost every class together and really enjoyed it. Participants talked about the importance of embracing the community and knowing what was going on in the computer science world as something they needed to learn to do. Positive Googler described the importance of the community this way:

> I think that if you went through the program and didn't talk to single person even if you got great grades I wouldn't consider that a success because I think that the community was a huge part of my experience and I think a huge part of the learning process.
>
> (Participant Positive Googler)

All six of the participants shared stories about the importance of personality and embracing the community and networking. One participant described feeling like she had gotten internships because she was not the stereotypical computer engineer. Dorm sister described realizing the importance of her community during her junior year; she said: "I mean there is tremendous support overall but doing well in [my classes] became a lot easier later on when I did get to know my classmates a lot more."

All six participants described enjoying the field because of its broad nature. One participant wishes she could have given her younger self the following piece of advice:

It's such a big field and there's so many different ways you can go with it and just reassuring myself that it's not like it's not specialized now but when it does get like more specific it will be more interesting. (Participant Theta Tau)

Finally, most of the participants wished they had had a better understanding of what computer science was, and what professional positions they could go into in industry, including job titles. Participants said they also would have liked a better description of the differences among the various computer science majors and what jobs each degree can prepare students for.

Reasons for Persisting

While the young women who participated in this study all described unique lived experiences, they all described having had a positive experience overall. Table 9 summarizes the themes from the research with respect to the reasons that participants gave for persisting in their major.

Table 9

Reasons for persisting in Computer Science and Engineering

Reason	Number of Participants Who Described It (Out of 6 Total)	Times Occurred
Interest	6	20
Positive Experience Overall	6	17
Female Peer Support: Emotional	6	15
Broad Content Area	6	14
Hard Worker	4	13
Positive Contribution to Society	4	10
Couldn't Imagine Doing Anything Else	5	9
Had Some Balance Outside of Major	3	6
Creative Process	4	4
Not Wanting to Quit	2	4
Never Considered Quitting	2	3
Stigma of Switching to Another Major	1	3

Note. The table was sorted based on times occurred.

Interest and strengths in STEM. All of the participants approached their undergraduate experience in diverse ways, and their journey to computer science was varied. One similarity for all of them was that they described their strengths in STEM subjects as high school students. All students also described positive experiences with their high school STEM teachers as contributing to their affinity for and persistence in those subjects. While one of the six participants had taken a programming class in high school, the other five participants did not have any programming experience. Of the five students who did not have any prior programming experiences, one declared a computer engineering major at Preview Day, one at orientation and the other three were encouraged to declare a computer engineering major after their first programming class in college. This first programming class was taught by a female professor who encouraged them to persist in the subject.

Wanting to help people. Four participants described the importance of making a positive contribution to society with their work. One participant described going into the field for this reason. She said:

> I knew that engineering you basically created something for society and whatnot. I was attracted to that aspect and actually being able to create something or create a product that's being used by everyone and really using it like math and science to do that.
>
> (Participant Dorm Sister)

Another participant, Robotics, described projects in her major this way: "I really liked those projects, I felt like I was making a difference and I wanted to like help people. I felt like I can do that through engineering so it's kind of why I went into engineering."

The important role of female peers, female mentors in general, and one mentor in particular. All participants described receiving support from their fellow female CSE majors. They described feeling comfortable working with their female peers and two talked about the valuable relationships that they had with a female near-peer mentor. For one student, this person was the same person who had influenced her to go into the school of engineering in the first place. The mentor had worked with her during an after-school outreach program. When this participant began her undergraduate experience, her near-peer mentor was a senior in the same department. The participant said that just knowing that this young woman had gone before her was very inspiring. She shared that simply being able to speak with or email this near-peer who had successfully completed the program she was attempting to complete was encouraging. Even though the two did not communicate much, this participant described her near-peer mentor as the reason she persisted when some of her male peers suggested she drop the major. She said:

> And I actually had some like male friends in the major be like yeah you should totally just stop now. And I was like no, I think I'll persevere. But having my mentor like seeing her, that she's at senior level, she's about to graduate she's made it that far, like [she] was, you know, just a good role model because I could see myself persevering and like staying until senior year so it was helpful to have an image of someone who's been successful and then even further was when she graduated and she went to Facebook I was like okay girls can do it. (Participant Technovation)

A different participant, White Hat, described a valuable experience with a different senior student who was enrolled in an upper division class that the participant took as an elective during her freshman year. The near-peer mentor had an internship at a well-known information security company and submitted the participant's resume for an internship that had opened up at her company. This experience influenced the rest of the participant's undergraduate experience as well as her early career.

Another participant, Dorm Sister, described having met an industry mentor at an event sponsored by a campus group. The industry mentor was described as having a positive influence on the participant who saw her mentor as a resource and role-model. She described her experience:

> [One panelist] was a computer engineer. She is on the cyber security team for NASA and when she talked about what she does I definitely was really interested. Afterwards I

just wanted to introduce myself to her and then we exchanged emails so I've kind of kept in touch with her ever since my first email. (Participant Dorm Sister)

While not all participants described having a relationship with a female peer or industry mentor, all six participants described the encouragement of a female professor as a key factor in having an overall positive experience. There was one female professor in particular that all participants described as key in encouraging each young woman's participation in the major. Students described her as someone who was committed to diversity issues and invested in seeing them succeed.

Behavior of helpful male peers. Participants described behavior from their male peers that made it easier for them to participate in the major. Technovation put it this way "I think the best ones aren't the ones who are like, 'yeah, women in tech,' but the ones that like treat me as an equal." Table 10 illustrates this supportive male peer behavior.

Table 10

Supportive Male Peer Behavior

Behavior	Number of Participants Who Described It (Out of 6 Total)	Times Occurred
Being Really Understanding	5	8
Being Aware of Language	5	6
Being Helpful Without Being Condescending	4	6
Making Sure Everyone Has the Opportunity to be Heard	4	5
Including Women in Friend Group	2	2

Note. The table was sorted based on times occurred.

One element, being aware of language, was mentioned above and reiterated by another participant this way:

Some of them are kind of like sensitive, to like when they know, like okay you're a girl, like I need to watch myself. Sometimes they don't. (Participant Technovation)

Another theme that was repeated by all of the participants was being included by the guys into their study groups and friend groups. One participant said:

I think the best thing is like including me into their group and I think that is also made possible by the groups at our school like ACM because even though there's the women's chapter like the just general ACM accepts women and men in the group and so that's just a good opportunity for them to like just be together and be friends. I wouldn't force any girls to befriend any boys, but I think it's a good way to feel like you're part of them and not just the other. (Participant Robotics)

Many participants mentioned feeling like they were the "other" when they weren't invited to participate in study or friend groups with their male peers. Not being condescending was another common recommendation for male peers from the participants. Five of the six participants had described at least one situation each in which a male peer was condescending to them. This theme was brought up ten times total in all of the interviews. Dorm Sister said, "Well they can first off be helpful without being condescending." Another participant stated that it would be helpful for her male peers not to question "us," as in females.

Another participant said:

Then for the ones that have been supportive like especially my close friends it's more like just it's really just like equal treatment I would say which is like the most supportive because even if you're like struggling in the class, like, they might also be struggling. And then, just being able to help each other out is nice because then you don't really feel like obviously it it's something that you do think about when there's only like a very limited number of females in the class. But, it's not like it doesn't feel as overwhelming if you have a good friend in the class that just sort of is there for you just because they actually want to help you not because... like oh it's because you're the only girl in the class, or oh it's because they need help. It's like, or they'll be the guy who may also need help from the female as well. (Participant Theta Tau)

Another described the same ideas this way:

> Just be super like transparent and like communicate clearly anything that like any questions you have or like I don't know. Like, I'd rather have like a very like upfront person and like I don't want them to think that like I don't know what I'm doing. And I want them to like treat me as equal and then just be like upfront. (Participant White Hat)

In describing what would be helpful in feeling included and welcomed by both her male peers and her male and female professors would be one participant said:

> Overall just creating a very inclusive environment, less of like a bro environment kind of. Umm, not just sitting with all your guy friends or when you have some projects or anything. Also, some of them kind of think that some of the women students are not doing as well just because we don't speak up. (Participant Dorm Sister)

Another participant put it this way:

> What I would try to try to address would be that [idea that] we're just as capable as any male of the same, like you know, brain caliber. And I think it is important to acknowledge that we might not have the same interests, we might not have the same um ways of thinking about things, but that doesn't make it any worse or better and to not assume certain things. (Participant Positive Googler)

Outside supports. Table 11 presents the outside supports that were described by participants as helpful during their time as undergraduates.

Table 11

Outside Supports

Support	Participants Who Described It (Out of 6 Total)	Times Occurred
Community Involvement: Outside of Major	5	12
Most College Friends Not in Major	4	6
Talked with Family	3	6
Hearing Another Female's Story	4	4
Sharing Story/Struggles in Confidence	3	4
Talked with Female Peers	3	3

(continued)

Support	Participants Who Described It (Out of 6 Total)	Times Occurred
Talked with Female Mentor (outside of school)	1	2
Talked with Male Peers	1	1
Talked with Male Mentor (outside of school)	0	0

Note. The table was sorted based on times occurred.

Five of the six participants described being involved in at least one undergraduate community at their university outside of their major. Four of the participants described most of their friends as being outside of their major. Robotics described not liking the competitive nature of her computer engineering friends and said: "My close friends aren't in my major ... and I personally like that because it doesn't feel like it's a competition. It doesn't feel like oh I'm taking this class and why aren't you taking this class or if we are taking the same class it's like oh I'm doing better than you."

Half of the participants described conversations with their family members as reassuring during their undergraduate experience. One participant described her constant, daily communication with her sister in order to get through her undergraduate experience. Female peer support and hearing the story of other females in computer science and engineering were described as helpful supports by participants. One participant described talking with a male peer as helpful and one other participant described her conversations with a female mentor outside of school as helpful.

Summary

Factors that encourage participation as well as factors that discourage participation for young women in computer science and engineering were described above. While all participants described unique experiences and reasons for persisting in their major, all six young women described having had a positive experience overall. Still, all six participants described experiencing imposter behavior and thoughts. These two themes were the two that participants described the most throughout all six interviews.

When asked about the elements that made computer science and engineering departments effective spaces for encouraging participation by females, all participants described: female professors mentoring and creating inclusive environments, the availability of professors, emotional support from female peers, additional news for women, and participation in the Grace Hopper Celebration. Of those themes, the ones described with the most frequency were female professors mentoring and creating inclusive environments, mentioned 23 times, and the availability of professors mentioned 17 times. Factors that made computer science and engineering departments ineffective spaces for encouraging participation by females were described with less frequency than the factors that encouraged participation. The three elements that were described most frequently by participants as discouraging their participation in their departments were condescending male peers, sexist language, and being treated differently as women.

The elements in their experiences that were described by participants as encouraging their participation were: their own interest in the topics, the broad content area, and their participation in study groups. The factors that discouraged their participation were described with less frequency and included: unsupportive male peers, being assigned menial tasks when working in groups with males, and unsupportive TAs. Another theme that was described a frequency of 19 times by all participants was the value of community and networking. Finally, when asked about their reasons for persisting in their major, all six participants described their interest in the subject area with a frequency of 20 times.

It is important to acknowledge that these themes were ones discussed by participants. While an interview protocol facilitated the interviews, participants had the freedom to guide the interview in whatever direction they wanted and discuss themes that they preferred while avoiding the ones they did not want to discuss. This chapter summarized the findings of the study. Chapter Five will discuss the significance of the findings and makes recommendations for further study.

Chapter Five: Conclusions and Suggestions for Future Research and Action

This chapter provides additional insights and recommendations from this qualitative study that explored how participants make sense of their personal lived experiences as women in undergraduate computer science and engineering departments. Part of this study investigated the role that research-based principles play in one undergraduate environment and relevant literature will be used to support the discussion. The chapter will be organized around the research questions and will include a description of the strengths and limitations of the study. Recommendations for future research and recommendations for practitioners will be identified. The chapter will conclude with the implications of the study.

Discussion of Key Findings

This study identified a number of themes that were commonly mentioned in the discussion around the experiences of participants during their undergraduate CSE experiences. All of the participants demonstrated resilient behavior as they persisted in their major while overcoming elements that might have discouraged their participation in the CSE major. Key findings are organized according to the research questions and are described below.

What are the lived experiences of female undergraduate computer science and engineering majors? During the interviews, participants focused on describing their experiences related to their identity as computer science and engineering majors and in most of the cases, did not discuss their lives or identities outside of the CSE major. Overall, participants described having had positive undergraduate CSE experiences, despite three of the students reporting harassment by a male professor in the department. This was not discussed in the findings to protect the identities of the students, and IRB was notified as described below on page 109. It is important to note that the women in this study were all "survivors" in that they were well over half-way done with their major. It is common for survivors to want to feel as good as they can about something they completed.

Five of the six participants began the major with limited knowledge about the computer science and engineering world both academically and socially. Participants described their understanding of this world as limited to the stereotypes pervasive in current media that are largely gendered representations of the tech world. These stereotypes are particularly prevalent in the gaming society and were described by Salter and Blodgett (2012) as a problematic area where sexism remains prevalent.

All of the participants in this study described knowing that they were going into a male-dominated field, but they also described not knowing what that meant. Schuster and Martiny (2016) describe the subtle sexism in math-related domains and the negative stereotypes that are powerful deterrents to the participation of women and result in their underrepresentation. While some of their female classmates did not remain in the major, the women in this study did. All of the participants described subtle and overt sexism and persisted in their major despite it for a variety of reasons described below.

None of the study participants felt prepared for their CSE courses and they described not knowing what the undergraduate CSE world was like nor what the industry options were for them after graduation. Despite four of the six participants describing feeling alone in their major and another four who reported feeling disconnected, all of the participants reported staying in the major because they felt like they had a good social network to support their progress. All four of the seniors described a special bond among the seven-total graduating female CSE students. Four participants described the positive collaboration and collaborative classroom experiences that they experienced with other women in the major; these experiences were important to them.

Despite their mostly positive overall experience in the CSE major, all of the participants described experiencing imposter behavior and thoughts. They questioned their successes and described not feeling like they deserved some of the opportunities they got, including internships and participation in hackathons. Experiences related to imposter behavior and thoughts will be described in more detail below in the section titled *imposter behavior and thoughts* that begins on page 109. This study illuminates the intersectional nature of the identity of female undergraduate CSE majors as well as the complex confluence of elements that contribute to their lived experience.

What types of experiences encourage participation and what makes undergraduate computer science and engineering departments effective spaces for encouraging the participation of female computer science and engineering undergraduates? This study found that growing a positive student community was essential for the persistence of these women in their major. All four of the seniors interviewed described the valuable connections that they made among the seven women total in their graduating class. The women supported one another and shared stories; they reported the group as being very collaborative and not competitive. They also described an understood level of confidentiality with the other women and they felt comfortable sharing both positive and negative experiences with their female friends in the CSE major.

Collaboration. A practice that lead to growing a positive student community for the participants of this study was their participation in study groups. Most participants described not being invited to male-only study groups and not being supported by some of their male peers in classes and in labs. The women in the study did form their own study groups and they also participated in the study groups of supportive male peers. When they worked with supportive male peers, they described the experience as a valuable one. One participant described study groups and supportive male and female classmates this way:

> It became a lot easier to do well in them because I was able to kind of get that additional support from my classmates. I keep going back to the importance of study groups and that's just because not only do you kind of get help from your classmates in terms of questions. But you're hearing questions that you would have thought about yourself and sort of bringing a whole other level to that studying and taking it a step further. So, my

computer science classes, doing well in them became a lot easier later on when I did get to know my classmates a lot more. (Participant Dorm Sister)

Female professors and mentors. Five of the six participants described having a female instructor who made an impact on them in their first programming course. They described this professor as an important factor in their decision to pursue their degree. This finding is consistent with the work of Beyer (2014) whose study found evidence for all students wanting to take more CS courses when they had excellent instructors. All of the participants described the invaluable support that they felt from one particular female faculty member (discussed as Female Mentor in Chapter 4). This finding supports the work by Stout and Camp (2014) that emphasizes the importance of students seeing role models who look "like them" as physical reminders that they too can be successful. The young women reported feeling a high level of comfort with this female professor, to the point where they and their other female classmates would go to her for academic and social support even when she had never taught them nor was their assigned advisor. The participants in the study credited this female professor with helping them overcome some of the challenges they faced as women in the major. This one female professor was instrumental in helping participants feel like they belonged in their major. This finding supports the work by Blaney and Stout (2017) who report that both self-efficacy and a sense of belonging are key predictors of retention, persistence, and success in the computing field. Other female and male professors were also described as supportive to the participants, but no other professor was mentioned by more than three participants in a positive way.

The supportive female professor (Female Mentor) organized a "women in engineering dinner" at the end of the term during finals week for the women in the department. The same professor also advised at least two student clubs the Association of Computing Machinery (ACM) general chapter as well as the women's chapter. These groups were described by the participants, with a few exceptions described in chapter four, as contributing to a positive student community. The student clubs were spaces where participants felt comfortable participating and they were also spaces where they were able to connect with women in the field through alumni and panel discussions.

Supportive male peers. Participants described the behavior of male peers as being both supportive and unsupportive. Supportive male peers were classmates who treated them equally, were aware to avoid gendered language, included the women in friend and study groups, and were helpful without being condescending. Supportive male peers were described as being aware of their language around the female students, and while this is important, the researcher noted that the young women who described this behavior implied that these male peers only watched their language around them and not when they were in male-only groups. As Technovation put it: "I think the best ones aren't the ones who are like yeah women in tech but the ones that like treat me as an equal." If that is, in fact, the case, then these male peers who were perceived as being supportive could still have been perpetuating negative stereotypes that might be gendered and contribute to non-inclusive environments for women.

Growing a positive student community and building student confidence. As described earlier, the research-based principles of the *Engagement Practices Framework* were used as an organizing framework for analyzing the results of this study. Two of the *Engagement Practices Framework* principles were described by all of the participants who talked about the valuable experience of participating in the Grace Hopper Celebration (GHC) at least once: growing a positive student community and building student confidence and professional identity. All of the participants described the value of learning more about the experiences of women who are currently in industry. Participants described seeing people at the conference who did not conform to the negative male-centric computer science world stereotypes as empowering. Seeing women they could identify with built their confidence and encouraged them to persist in the field. All participants experienced the Grace Hopper Celebration as having a lasting impact that helped them develop their identities as female computer engineers and remain positive when things became difficult. One participant described it this way:

I wish I [had gone] every year because it was such an awesome experience. I thought it was so empowering, I left feeling amazing. Just to see all these women pursuing similar career paths and it was just really encouraging. Yeah, it was a really great experience. (Participant Technovation)

Participants reported that GHC was also a place where they began to dispel the male centered CS-world stereotypes, see people they could relate to, and build their professional identities. Theta Tau described the value of GHC as a place where she was "able to look around and sort of know that the people around have this mindset that we all belong in computing." Participants also described the value of being able to talk with women in the field and begin to figure out what career(s) they might want to have. Participants shared that the panels at GHC as well as the career fair as being particularly helpful. When it comes to building confidence, the researcher found that this exposure to the community and to computer science and technology-related career opportunities was important for participants.

Curriculum and Pedagogy. Another finding of this study is the importance of sound pedagogical approaches in addition to relevant content. The third research-based principle of the *Engagement Practices Framework* is making the content matter. Participants illustrated this principle when talked about wanting to take more CS courses when they had excellent professors who used pedagogically sound practices. This finding is consistent with the work of Beyer (2014) whose study found evidence for the value of good pedagogical practices in attracting and retaining students in CS. The participants in this study described learning experiences that encouraged their participation, including professors who really cared about the material they were teaching, engaging material, relevant examples and problems, and opportunities to practice and apply concepts. This idea can be summed up with this statement by Dorm Sister who said: "I think the professor matters just as much if not more than the content that they're teaching." This idea supports the finding by other researchers that having good instructors, given the difficulty level of CS, is important for the success of students.

All of the participants in this study pointed to their labs and practice problems as helpful, as were instructional strategies that allowed them to apply concepts through relevant and interesting assignments. They described the value of a curriculum that was grounded in reality and that reflects what is being done in the "real world." This finding is consistent with the work of Monge et al. (2015) who described the importance of relevant practice problems in the *Engagement Practices Framework*. Another instructional approach that two participants described as having been very helpful was pair programming. This finding is consistent with the work of Werner and Denning (2009) who found that while working with a partner, girls engaged in exploratory talk involving metacognitive monitoring of themselves and their partners. For one of the participants, pair programming was the first opportunity she had to work with a male peer and gauge her programming abilities. She described feeling like she had gotten an opportunity to prove to her male peer that she belonged in the major. Her reasoning demonstrates the prevalence of the stereotypes of the field, and this is problematic. Whether consciously or subconsciously, the participant who feels she has to prove herself can perpetuate the stereotypes that were possibly reinforced through her participation in the major. Participants acknowledged the importance of their professors and peers avoiding stereotypes in their behavior as well as in their language.

Building awareness of computer science and engineering. Most of the participants described wishing they had known more about the different CS-related majors and career opportunities in those fields earlier. This is consistent with the findings of Alvarado and Dodds (2010) who described three practices that succeeded in increasing the number of women in computer science at Harvey Mudd College. The practices are: (a) recruiting even before students arrive on campus and actively through the first semester and year, (b) hands-on programs that challenge and stretch students, and (c) a top-down curricular focus that emphasizes the reality – not the stereotype – of CS. Participants described being recruited actively by professors during preview days (before school started), orientation, and throughout the first year. The participants confirmed research that suggests that the first undergraduate courses were key intervention points for attracting and retaining members of underrepresented groups, specifically women to the fields of computer science and engineering (Alvarado & Dodds, 2010; Monge et al., 2015). Participants described the important role of their first CS courses as well as professors in their decision to pursue the major. Five of the participants described having a female professor for their first CS course and they described this professor as supportive and encouraging of their pursuit of the major even after they finished the course.

What types of experiences discourage participation and what makes undergraduate computer science and engineering departments ineffective spaces for encouraging the participation of female computer science and engineering undergraduates? As described above, there are myriad elements that discourage the participation of women in undergraduate computer science and engineering spaces. Some of these elements included: subtle and overt sexism, perpetuating negative stereotypes through language and/or behavior, access, and not seeing themselves reflected in the field – resulting in young women experiencing imposter behavior and thoughts.

Harassment. As mentioned above, this study uncovered a reportable sexual harassment offense that had gone unreported. The researcher did report the offense to IRB. While the details of this unsolicited harassment will not be described here, the incident raises questions about the persistence of harassment in the field. Harassment continues to be an issue that young women face in this field and it is unclear why incidents of harassment often goes unreported. It could be that the student respects the person harassing her, she might see them as a role model, she might believe that it is normal behavior, or she might need this person to give her a positive recommendation for a leadership role or for a job. More research needs to be done to better understand how to ensure that this behavior is not normalized.

Imposter behavior and thoughts. One common finding that discouraged the building of student confidence and professional identity was the description of imposter behavior and thoughts by all participants. Participants repeatedly described their awareness of the low number of females in the field and how that lead to their feelings of both imposter behavior as well as stereotype threat. This finding supports the work of Beyer (2014) who described stereotype threat as a phenomenon whereby stereotypes can produce performance impairment. In CS-related fields, the lack of female representation can undermine the sense of belonging and performance of women in it.

One participant described how GHC helped her push through these feelings:

I think a lot of times when classes are hard I question if I'm doing the right major, like oh gosh is it too late switch now? But [being at GHC] is reassuring because yes, this major is hard like you will struggle through it. And obviously for women it's sort of a different experience especially if for example like if you don't see like another woman necessarily like in the field or like a certain role you want. (Participant Theta Tau)

This finding supports the work of Falkner, et al. (2015) who described imposter thoughts as being gendered. However, one participant did describe her male peers as also experiencing imposter thoughts. Falkner, et al. (2015) described providing a clear, positive message about what computer science is as one way to mitigate imposter thoughts and behaviors. The participants in this study wished they had gotten a better definition of the various computer science and engineering degrees at their school, including degree requirements and career options upon graduation. Participants thought that this information would have been most helpful before they started their major. By giving more information to students earlier, it might be possible to mitigate some of the negative media-driven stereotypes that could otherwise be the focus for young people who have no other exposure to the field. This finding echoed the research by Falkner, et al. (2015) that recommends giving a complete picture of what the CS entails, not just the technical piece.

Lack of early exposure. The participants in this study described wishing that they had had more exposure to CS before college. They described having to work hard to catch up and they also described the additional pressure that resulted in their lack of confidence in their classes. This supports previous research that shows that previous programming experience might contribute to a sense of confidence for undergraduate students just starting off (Horton & Craig, 2015; Wilson & Shrock, 2001). Stoilescu and Egodawatte (2010) describe a lack of prior experience and exposure to CS as an issue that affects females more than males. This study supports the assertion that lack of experience is an obstacle for women and one that might deter some from the field. One participant described it this way:

> When I got into it freshman year everyone was so far ahead of me and I just felt really intimidated. I was like I don't know what this is, I don't know what this means. It didn't stop me from trying really hard, but I feel like I felt more pressure to do better and I feel like I can see like people getting deterred from that. (Participant Positive Googler)

Digital divides. All but one participant described the digital divides discussed in the research including a lack of access to CS-related materials and instruction before college. This divide lead to a lack of access to the computing culture prior to college except for the negative stereotypes that persist about the field. This finding is related to the work of Medel and Pournaghshband (2017) that describes established male-centered representation in computer science curriculum materials including imagery, language, examples, and other content. All of these issues including the lack of prior experience and exposure to CS seems to have contributed to the disparity of participation between female and male students in this undergraduate program.

Negative stereotypes. Another common finding that discouraged the building of student confidence and professional identity was professors and classmates who perpetuated negative computer science world stereotypes. This study found this to be an ongoing problem and supports previous findings by Stoilescu and McDougall (2011) who reported that female students view CS as a hostile culture and environment. This study also supports the finding from the Stoilescu and McDougall (2011) study that male students were more active in classrooms and more likely to receive attention from teachers and administrators. For example, participants in this study described behavior by both male and female professors that perpetuates the view that CS is a male domain. This behavior included that of unsupportive male peers who double-checked the answers of their female peers in class, harassed female professors, overpowered their female peers in class, made sexist comments, assigned menial tasks to women when working in groups, and reinforced negative CS-world stereotypes. Participants described TAs (who were all described as male) and both male and female professor behavior as reinforcing negative CS-world stereotypes. These elements did not support the development of a positive student community. One recommendation to mitigate this problem would be to recruit and train young women to serve as TAs for undergraduate courses. This recommendation is further described below in the section titled *female peer and mentor support*. Surprisingly, though the female students reported negative stereotypes and issues, they did not seem to want to dwell on the problems.

Outside interests. The literature documents how female CS-related majors describe having interests outside of just the computer and programing; they lack an interest in complete immersion into the "computer science world." The computer science world stereotype, then, eroded the confidence and sense of belonging in the undergraduate CS community for some women leading them to doubt their belonging in the community (Margolis, Fisher, & Miller, 1999). Beck (2007) reports that a majority of men in undergraduate CS programs describe themselves as computer nerds, geeks, and hackers, while female participants do not detach themselves from people or social concerns; rather, these were essential components of their identity. The researchers reported the perception by women of the male-centered world as limiting and machine-centered. Several participants in this study confirmed this research by describing the hours they would spend away from the computers in their spare time. One participant described noticing that during her summer internships, when she was programming all day, she would come home and craft the rest of the day or all weekend. She described needing crafting to balance out the time she spent programming at the computer at work. Another participant described being okay programming all day as long as it was not every day. However, two of the participants described the need to work on side projects in order to be successful computer science engineers. Positive Googler described it this way "To be successful you should take on a side [computing] project or you should, you know, spend some more time outside of school doing it." One question that has come up as a result of this research is whether there is a true need to take on a side computing project – in addition to programming all day at school or work.

Strengths and Limitations

This study is a small contribution to the knowledge base on the experiences of women in undergraduate CS-related programs. A small number of students at one U.S. university participated in this study and its findings cannot be generalized to the experiences of women in computer science and engineering undergraduate programs at this school nor at universities as a whole. Nor can the findings be generalized to the experiences of women in all CS-related undergraduate programs. One limitation faced by this study is the low number of females in computer science and engineering undergraduate programs that has been documented above. Furthermore, convenience sampling restricted participation to participants who were available, chose to participate, or were encouraged to participate by another study participant. Participants also had to be young women in their junior or senior year majoring in computer science and engineering. Young women who left the major prior to their junior or senior year were excluded from the study.

Participants in the study were willing to provide thoughtful and thorough responses to the interview questions. As a result, the researcher compiled a rich and detailed account of the lived experiences of these women as they answered interview questions focused on gaining a better understanding of what it was like for to be a female undergraduate computer science and engineering major and the experiences that encouraged or discouraged their participation. It is important to recognize a limitation of the research methods employed, which is that participants were free to guide the interview in different directions and focus on the elements that they wanted to focus on. In this study, participants described more positive experiences than negative ones. It is unclear if participants described a more positive experience overall experience because that was the case or if they did not want to share or did not feel comfortable sharing more of their negative experiences. Also, participants did not discuss all of themes that were described in the literature. There can be a variety of reasons for this including, once again, the limitations of the research methods chosen for this study.

As a result of the limited number of females in this undergraduate major at this school, the study is affected by sampling bias, including self-selection as well as survivorship bias. Survivorship bias has been described by Smith (2014) as a cognitive bias that occurs when only those who have survived past a certain point are considered or studied. While the study represented over 50% of the females in the senior class, it represented a much lower percentage of the females in the junior class. Finally, this study included a racial and ethnically diverse group of women, but it did not include any Latina or White women, resulting in further limitations to its broad applicability.

Recommendations for Practitioners

Wang et al. (2015) describe the factors playing a role in a young woman's decision to pursue a CS-related degree in college as largely controllable. This means that practitioners, along with family and friends, can play a significant positive role in encouraging and exposing young women in CS-related fields. This study illuminated some recommendations that might guide the work of practitioners in secondary school as well as higher education.

Early exposure and dispelling stereotypes. One recommendation was to give students, especially those just starting their programs or deciding among several CS and Engineering programs a clear description of each one of the programs as well as what career paths in each look like. Participants thought that understanding career paths would have been most helpful before they started their major confirming the research of Wang et al. (2015). As described in chapter three, she enters college, CS degree and class requirements can be overwhelming to female undergraduates. Furthermore, young women are often interested in more than "just programming computers;" they tend to be interested in creating computing tools to help society. It is important to show young women that CS is a field with diverse applications and a broad potential for positive societal impacts because of the value that women place on making positive contributions to society. As mentioned above, one recommendation is to better understand the importance of side projects for computer science and engineering students. Is the commonly shared advice to take on a side project in addition to programming all day at school or work really important? Furthermore, it might be important for practitioners to support students in taking a break from programming and engage in activities outside of the CS world. Helping students understand that identity does not just have to be about CS and engineering is a message that students in this study might have benefited from.

Early exposure. Also, this study shows the importance of exposure to the field. Students who took one CS class were more likely to want to pursue CS. When it comes to gender, Wang and Moghadam (2017) found that while there is no difference in access to computers or CS learning opportunities for young women and men, there is less awareness of opportunities and less encouragement by adults. Girls are less likely to know about clubs, online sites, or other opportunities outside of school to learn CS. Boys are more likely than girls to learn CS on their own, in a group or club, and online. It is important for secondary school practitioners to expose students to programming and other computer science learning opportunities. Educators and people in the lives of young women play a large role in providing opportunities for them to learn about these fields and their participation.

Female peer and mentor support. Encouraging young women to support one another and setting up the conditions for both peer, near-peer, and mentor support to happen is essential. This can also be done by exposing young women to participants in the field. It can also be done in the form of on-campus clubs, off-campus clubs, conferences, and other activities. The literature documents how women often do not see themselves reflected in a male-centered computer science world. Telling the stories of women in computer science and helping women see themselves reflected in the field is an important step in encouraging the participation of women in CS (Gürer, 2002). Having more women in leadership roles in computer science and engineering departments might help change the traditional computer science world stereotype. A stereotype that has been found to erode the confidence and sense of belonging for some women leading them to doubt their belonging in the undergraduate community (Margolis, Fisher, & Miller, 1999). Recruiting and training female TAs to work with all students in undergraduate courses might help create more inclusive learning environments. All students would see women as leaders and near-peer mentors and young women could have more exposure to people who look like them in the field.

All participants in this study reported participation in department-sponsored events as essential to their overall positive experience in the major. These opportunities take time and energy on the part of someone and it is important to have practitioners appropriately compensated for these efforts. Participants described their experiences in spaces where they felt supported as essential in helping them develop their individual identities as members of the CSE community. An element that is essential to creating spaces where all feel included is explicit education in dealing with social and emotional situations that might come up specifically for women in these CS-related spaces and communities. One recommendation that was not described as already being available to students in the study is to provide role-playing and training opportunities to help young women understand how to deal with situations they might experience in the field, including gender bias, stereotypes, microaggressions, and sexual harassment. The young women who participated in this study came from a wide range of backgrounds and all of them might have benefited from explicit education and training in these topics.

Role of professors and mentors. For professors who work in undergraduate programs, it is essential that they continue to push back against the traditional CS world stereotypes. Training for professors, staff, and mentors might be needed to help everyone understand potential blind spots and the ways in which they might be unconsciously perpetuating negative stereotypes. It might be necessary for professors to speak with their colleagues or even report their colleagues who might not be aware that they are perpetuating stereotypes, or even worse, actively making students feel uncomfortable by acting inappropriately. It is the responsibility of community members to ensure a safe space for students and training to that effect might be necessary and prudent in some cases. Ultimately, it is essential to help all students feel welcomed and included in computer science and engineering communities, and the undergraduate communities that they encounter are important places to begin creating inviting spaces.

Recommendations for Future Research

This study was limited to better understanding the lived experiences of young women enrolled in one computer science and engineering undergraduate program in the United States. More studies of the experiences of women in CS-related undergraduate programs at schools across the United States and the world are necessary in order to better understand this phenomenon. Furthermore, it is important to study the experiences of the women who dropped out of the Computer Science and Engineering undergraduate major at any point during their undergraduate program. Their experiences are essential in understanding the factors that might have contributed to their decision to leave the major.

Researchers should take a closer look at the qualities that make up a "successful" computer engineer at various points in the education and industry landscapes. For example, as described above, two participants in this study described the need to take on a side project – in addition to programming all day at school or work. This is something that the young women in this study described as difficult for them because they did not want to spend all of their free time programming. They wanted to be able to pursue other interests and for one in particular, pursuing crafting as opposed to programming more was essential to her overall well-being. So, an area for further research is the degree to which side projects or full immersion into the computer science world is necessary and to what degree participants in this world should or need to take breaks from it in order to participate successfully in it. Another way of putting it is are there degrees of participation or immersion in the computer science world that can afford participants in the landscape equal preparation for approaching computer engineering problems in their work environments?

Another line of research that emerges from this study is a closer examination of the experiences of female professors at these institutions. Specifically, it would be interesting to study the factors that make their experiences effective or ineffective as well as the amount of additional time that they might spend informally mentoring and advising students who are not formally assigned to them. Yet another important line of research is to study the behavior of professors who do not perpetuate the view that CS is a male domain as well as those who do. Raising awareness of problematic behavior is one step in stopping it. Understanding the behavior and habits of professors might help others learn to mitigate their own behaviors and to create more inclusive learning environments for all of their students. It is important to understand the role of professors of both genders who do not conform to the traditional male-centric computer science world stereotypes and who have been identified by female students as supportive professors or advisors. Their experience within the complex system of their department would be fascinating to study. Another related thread is gaining better understanding of how TAs are chosen and trained since this work might also lead to environments that encourage the participation of more diverse groups.

The findings of this study cannot be generalized to the experiences of women in all CS-related undergraduate programs. As a result, future work with other methodologies, such as a survey, can build on the insights from this work and lead to a more general understanding of the experiences of women in CS-related undergraduate programs. This might lead to gathering data from a larger number of females in Computer Science and Engineering undergraduate programs. It would be interesting to ask questions like: How does the number of women in a department relate to the success of women in that department? How does the number of female professors in a department relate to the number and/or success of women in that department?

Finally, understanding the experiences of pre-college girls in CS courses or afterschool activities is important. It is important to find ways to set up young women and other underrepresented groups for success in the tech world through mitigating stereotype threat, dispelling negative and pervasive CS worldviews, and providing images of the positive and exciting elements of the CS world. While in an ideal world, women and underrepresented groups would not have to deal with negative experiences, the unfortunate reality is that they do. One way to mitigate this might be to study how to effectively provide young women with the tools to stand up for themselves and deal with microaggressions and other negative experiences that might come up. More research needs to be done to understand what to do and how to do it. It is also important to provide support and platforms to women in post-graduate programs and in industry so that they can then share their stories and provide support to the next generation of women.

Implications

The findings of this study support previous studies investigating the participation of females and other underrepresented minorities in CS-related fields. The participants in this study described elements of their experience as a CSE major that perpetuate the view that CS is a male domain and other negative stereotypes. Participants also described behavior that was hostile and discouraged their participation in the culture. While some terrible stories came to light as a result of this study, the participants all described having an experience that was more positive than negative. The specific strategies that the women in this study identified as helpful during their undergraduate experiences included: family, faculty, and peer support; feeling a connection to the CS culture; a supportive learning environment; informal and formal mentors; interest in STEM subjects and in CSE in particular; and a resounding need to make a positive impact on society. All participants persisted in the major in part because they saw it as a way to make a positive contribution to society.

This study makes it clear that more work needs to be done in this space. That work is outlined above in the recommendations for practitioners and recommendations for future research sections. This study also implies that there is reason to remain hopeful that positive advances can be made in the field to make it more welcoming for groups that are currently underrepresented.

Closing Thoughts

Young women need more access to role-models who are able to dispel the existing computer science world stereotypes. This study illuminated the essential role that one female professor in this CSE program played in the experience of all six participants. This professor had a far-reaching influence on these young women in a variety of areas related to both education and social support. It is clear that undergraduate CS departments need professors, whether male or female, who can connect with students and are seen by those students as someone who is invested in their progress and success.

The young women who participated in this study approached their undergraduate experience in diverse ways. Their unique personalities allowed them to interpret their experiences in their own way. And, while all students described negative experiences in their undergraduate experiences, some did not have the social-emotional tools to deal with the experiences that they unfortunately faced. Having to put up with microaggressions or proving their worth, however, is part of the problem with the current reality of the CS and tech worlds. In 1975, Toni Morrison described the divisiveness of this type of problem in relationship to race this way:

> The function, the very serious function of racism is distraction. It keeps you from doing your work. It keeps you explaining, over and over again, your reason for being. Somebody says you have no language and you spend twenty years proving that you do. Somebody says your head isn't shaped properly so you have scientists working on the fact that it is. Somebody says you have no art, so you dredge that up. Somebody says you have no kingdoms, so you dredge that up. None of this is necessary. There will always be one more thing. (Portland State University, May 30, 1975)

Getting to a point where gender (and race) is not a distraction that keeps women from doing their work is essential. In his recent article in the Atlantic, Bogost (2017) addressed the conditions that produce and perpetuate systemic inequities in the tech field. He concluded his article with these lines:

> Reader, I want so desperately to leave you with an alternative. A better option, a new strategy. One that would anticipate and defang the inevitable maws crying, "Well, what's your solution, then?" But facile answers spun off-the-cuff by white men in power—aren't these the things that brought trouble in the first place?

Conclusions

The purpose of this qualitative phenomenological study was to look at how participants make sense of their lived experiences as women in undergraduate computer science and engineering departments. Through semi-structured one-on-one interviews, the researcher explored the meanings that participants linked to their experiences. While this study confirmed that some stereotypes, biases, microaggressions, and discrimination continue to pervade the "CS world," it also included hopeful findings. All of the participants described unique lived experiences. Nevertheless, all six of the participants described having had a positive experience overall. Participants described the value of opportunities to apply concepts through practice, labs, and relevant and interesting assignments. All of the participants described the value of social supports including the support of female professors, female role models, supportive peers of both genders, the availability of professors, and study groups as contributing to a positive learning community. All of the students described the importance of hearing other females' stories as well as having benefited from seeing someone ahead of them in industry or in school. The Grace Hopper Celebration was described as a place where participants were able to see themselves reflected in the participants and they were able to see that a CS identity can take many forms.

In closing, this study suggests hope for the CS and tech communities. It is a small contribution to recent efforts to broaden the story and the history of these communities by illuminating the lived experiences of women and telling their stories. It confirmed the importance of continuing the work to dispel stereotypes and to illuminate the experiences of women and other underrepresented groups in the field. Everybody deserves a more aware, inclusive, cooperative, and inviting "computer science world" that treats them as equals – after all, that is what the young women in this study repeatedly asked for. For the researcher in particular, this study marks another step in her efforts to encourage a diverse group of people to pursue and persist in the tech landscape.

www.ingramcontent.com/pod-product-compliance
Lightning Source LLC
LaVergne TN
LVHW011954070526
838202LV00054B/4913